JESSIE'S
Corner

Something To Think About

Becky Gillette

WESTBOW
PRESS®
A DIVISION OF THOMAS NELSON
& ZONDERVAN

WestBow Press books may be ordered through booksellers or by contacting:

WestBow Press
A Division of Thomas Nelson & Zondervan
1663 Liberty Drive
Bloomington, IN 47403
www.westbowpress.com
844-714-3454

Because of the dynamic nature of the Internet, any web addresses or links contained in this book may have changed since publication and may no longer be valid. The views expressed in this work are solely those of the author and do not necessarily reflect the views of the publisher, and the publisher hereby disclaims any responsibility for them.

Any people depicted in stock imagery provided by Getty Images are models, and such images are being used for illustrative purposes only. Certain stock imagery © Getty Images.

Interior image credits:
Phyllis Brack from Dilly & Doc Creative Studio, Great Bend, Kansas

This book is a work of non-fiction. Unless otherwise noted, the author and the publisher make no explicit guarantees as to the accuracy of the information contained in this book and in some cases, names of people and places have been altered to protect their privacy.

Unless otherwise indicated, all Scripture quotations are taken from THE MESSAGE, copyright © 1993, Scripture quotations marked NIV are taken from the Holy Bible, New International Version®, NIV®. Copyright © 1973, 1978, 1984 by Biblica, Inc.™ Used by permission of Zondervan. All rights reserved worldwide.

Scripture quotations marked NKJV are taken from the New King James Version. Copyright © 1982 by Thomas Nelson, Inc. Used by permission. All rights reserved.

Scripture quotations marked AMP are taken from the Amplified® Bible, Copyright © 1954, 1958, 1962, 1964, 1965, 1987 by The Lockman Foundation. Used by permission

Unless otherwise indicated, all Scripture quotations are taken from THE MESSAGE, copyright © 1993, 2002, 2018 by Eugene H. Peterson. Used by permission of NavPress. All rights reserved. Represented by Tyndale House Publishers, Inc.

ISBN: 978-1-6642-9986-3 (sc)
ISBN: 978-1-6642-9987-0 (hc)
ISBN: 978-1-6642-9985-6 (e)

Library of Congress Control Number: 2023908997

Print information available on the last page.

WestBow Press rev. date: 06/26/2023

Contents

Spring

Summer

Fall

Winter

Preface

Several years ago, I decided to read the Bible from back to front. I discovered that I had read the Bible from front to back so many times that I was anticipating the next verses and not really paying attention to what they said.

I started in Revelation 22 and read a chapter at a time, writing down one passage from each chapter that caught my eye. I kept all these passages in a file box and, in 2019, when I started working for a small weekly newspaper, I decided to put them to use. I randomly chose twelve passages—one for each week of a season—and, using the order in which they were drawn from the file box, wrote a column called "Jessie's Corner" for the paper.

At the time, I had three cats who would listen to my questions and, with a tilt of their heads or a smile on their faces, they would encourage me to keep talking, to find a path through the wilderness of life that led me closer to God and an acceptance of his mysterious ways. This book is named for my middle cat, Jessie, who stuck with me through many confusing twists and turns. This is why there's a cat on the cover.

I prefer to call these pieces meditations rather than devotions because they are intended to give people something to think about. I do not have any authority to tell you what you must or must not believe. My intent is to introduce you to the God that I love. God has created so much diversity, and the tendency is for people to feel more comfortable with the familiar. Many of us, however, do not fit into the safe, comfortable traditions. There is hope for us also. God loves each of us with an unswerving intensity, and we need to be aware of that.

When I was a young woman, I was invited to attend an adult Sunday school class whose members were people of great intellect and religious background. They included doctors, a lawyer, several oil executives, farmers, and a few wives. The topic under discussion was Judgment Day, and their pronouncement was that, on that fearsome day, we would all be required to stand before God and account for our actions.

In a moment of amazing bravery, my mom spoke up and noted that God already knew the actions we had taken and why. She suggested that we become friends with God, and that way, we would know him personally and, trusting him, we wouldn't be so afraid. There was a moment of silence in the room, and that event became etched in my mind.

Ever since then, I have invited God to join with me in everything I do. I want to know him as much as I possibly can. *Friend* is a word with many connotations. We have acquaintances who are called "friends" just because they aren't exactly enemies. We have "friends" that we maintain because they can be counted on to provide something we need—social intelligence, how to get stains out of laundry, or just a sounding board.

The kind of friend that is available to us in the triune God is deeper and more profound than any friendship I have ever found. I find myself talking to him about any topic, and he has helped me find answers to crossword puzzles as well as to trickier questions involving the universe. He has become my best friend, and I would like to introduce you to him.

Acknowledgments

Thank you to:

Justin—because I said I would,

Betty, Kathie, Karen, Joanne, and Phyllis for their encouragement and support (and because they laughed in all the right places),

the congregations where I have served in the pulpit for sharing their wisdom with me, and

my best friend, without whom this would not be possible. Thank you, God!

Bible translations used:

New International Version
New King James Version
The Amplified Bible
The Message

Spring

While you are welcome to start these meditations at any point in the year, there is a cycle to life that can provide a comforting foundation to our lives. Spring is a time of new growth, a time of fresh starts. It is the first season that falls totally within one year.

Spring is a time of childhood when we can explore the world around us, making discoveries of great importance—the day we discover our toes, or we learn the joy of eating ice cream.

Spring is a never-ending time of play, punctuated by periods of time spent in a classroom learning how to formulate the "correct" answers to questions that have no meaning—yet.

All too soon, however, childhood moves into young adulthood, and we become more responsible for our own choices. Spring moves into summer.

Getting Married

"Let us celebrate, let us rejoice, let us give him the glory! The Marriage of the Lamb has come; his Wife has made herself ready. She was given a bridal gown of bright and shining linen. The linen is the righteousness of the saints" (Revelation 19:7–8).

Weddings and marriages are two different things. Weddings are filled with promises and hope. It is anticipated that marriages will be the fulfillment of those promises and that hope.

Wherever there's a wedding, there is hope that we won't be traveling through life alone, that there will be someone who sees us and will stick by us, covering our backs. There is a promise that we will be able to leave something of ourselves for the future. It is a forward-looking day!

Weddings are sparkling! It doesn't matter if you have an extravagant gown and formal tuxedo or a comfortable shirt and jeans. It doesn't matter if you have a string orchestra playing in the background or a jukebox. You can have twelve attendants or only the two of you. There is a shine to weddings. Most everyone's happy, with the possible exception of a few jealous or disgruntled people who wandered in by mistake!

Weddings are cozy or luxurious. You may have the wedding at your house, in a cathedral, or on a Caribbean island. You may have the wedding in a meadow, in a forest, by a lake, or in a courthouse. Weddings are about sharing an important moment with someone else.

Very few people have a wedding with the expectation that the marriage will not last. Even people having a wedding for purposes other than deep love—for dynasties, maybe, or to gain citizenship—have a hope that something bigger may come from this. There is something within us that is looking for the happy ending—no matter how cynical we may have become. That is faith! Hope springs eternal.

We celebrate weddings because two people are willing to take on the future! Anymore, the future looks a little bleak. There are fewer weddings now, or maybe the weddings take place later in the relationships. Many people are trying to hedge their bets, thinking that if they can stay together for a year or so, maybe they'll be able to stay together for a long time! Weddings are a sign that these two people are taking a gamble that they will be able to overcome the odds and make their relationship last forever.

Not everyone wins that gamble, but that doesn't stop many of us from trying again and again. With the vision of a good marriage imprinted within us, we strive to find that for ourselves.

Jesus's first miracle was at a wedding—in Cana! He turned water into wine. Not because these people were especially good or religious but because they were friends of his mom's, and she didn't want them embarrassed! You have to love a God like that!

If there is anyone who should have hope for the future, it's the children of God! The marriage of the Lamb and his bride, the church, should be quite a celebration! It will be an event not to be missed!

Bloom Where You're Planted

"As Jesus was getting into the boat, the demon-delivered man begged to go along, but he wouldn't let him. Jesus said, "Go home to your own people. Tell them your story—what the Master did, how he had mercy on you." The man went back and began to preach in the Ten Towns area about what Jesus had done for him. He was the talk of the town" (Mark 5:18–20).

It seems that there was a fellow who lived in a cemetery, and nothing or nobody could control him. They chained him and tied him up with ropes, but he kept breaking free. He would meander around, screaming and cutting himself. One day, he saw Jesus out walking, and he ran up, telling Jesus to leave him alone. This fellow was tired of people trying to change him, and he didn't want anyone else getting in his way.

Does this sound familiar? How many times do we get tired of people trying to "improve" us? We're just fine the way we are, thank you very much! If one more person tries to tell me how to fix my hair or how to dress, I'm liable to punch them in the nose!

Jesus asks for this fellow's name. He sees this fellow, who says that he is filled with demons. Jesus sends the demons into a herd of pigs, and they run over a cliff and die. The people who owned the pigs demand that Jesus leave the area and never come back! (He didn't help their business very much by killing all the livestock.) Jesus gets into a boat to leave, and this is when the fellow asks to go with him.

It's odd, but when we know that someone sees us for who we are, we can lose the chip on our shoulder! When I think that someone is expecting me to be perfect, I can start acting badly. If I understand that they just expect me to be myself, I lose a lot of aggression. I can become nice! I think this is what happened to the person from the cemetery. Jesus saw him for who he was—without the demons.

I think that the fellow was a little scared that Jesus was the only one who saw him as nice, and he probably wanted to stay close to Jesus for security. But Jesus says, "No, you can handle this!" Jesus tells the fellow to talk about what happened to him and how he was affected.

We need to tell our stories as honestly as we can. The more we tell our stories, the more comfortable we can become in our own skin and the more we can help others go through the same situations. When someone comes along to tell us that we're wrong, we can smile at them nicely and know that they don't have a clue. It might save a nose or two!

Save Your Energy

"They turned on Paul and Barnabas and forced them to leave. Paul and Barnabas shrugged their shoulders and went on to the next town, Iconium, brimming with joy and the Holy Spirit, two happy disciples" (Acts 13:52 MSG).

There is a law in thermodynamics that is familiar to most everyone. It says that energy can't be destroyed, only converted. The idea is that there is a certain amount of energy in the universe. We can't create more energy, and we can't destroy it. All we can do is convert it. We can take the energy in the food we eat and transfer it to our bodies so that we can think and move and clean house! It would be nice to find a way to convert the energy of a toddler (or two). We could probably light up a small country with that much energy!

Paul and Barnabas were in Antioch of Pisidia one Sunday, visiting the local church. The leader of the congregation made the mistake of asking them if they had any words for the people. Paul stood up and started talking about Jesus.

The leaders of the area started telling the important people of the town that Paul and Barnabas were rabble-rousers—out to destroy the way of life that they loved. As a result, Paul and Barnabas were asked to leave.

I don't think that there is anyone who has not been asked to leave somewhere. We start to confide in someone who we consider a friend, they take offense at what we say, and we don't hear from them again. We are sitting at our desk, doing our job, and the boss comes along and says that we are no longer providing good service, and he asks us to pack up our stuff, walk out the door, and never come back.

Usually, what happens is that we feel betrayed, angry, sad, disappointed, and uncertain of the future! Often, we spend time in front of a mirror or with others, hashing and rehashing the experience until it's been pureed and can be served like baby food! Our energy is converted to anger—and not just anger but impotent anger that does nothing except stir up our stomachs so that we make ourselves sick.

Matthew, Mark, and Luke all talk about visiting others. They all say something to the effect that, if the house offers you peace, accept it. It if doesn't, shake the dust off your shoes and walk away, taking your peace back.

We have kids, bosses, neighbors, friends, couches, books, and pets who are clamoring for our attention. If we don't feel good when we are around all these, we should stop going around them. That's not always easy to do when it's your own family who steals your peace.

Life is a fine balancing act between taking care of our families and taking care of ourselves. This may be why spas are so popular! Amid chaos, we need to find a place where we can be at peace. That's why bathrooms have locks!

Into the Wild

"Now Jesus, full of the Holy Spirit, left the Jordan and was led by the Spirit into the wild" (Luke 4:1).

John baptized Jesus in the Jordan River, and God announced that He was well pleased by his son. Jesus was about thirty when he started public life. There isn't much said about Jesus from the time he was born to the time when he started his ministry. The only time when we hear about Jesus as a boy is when he was twelve and stayed to question the rabbis in Jerusalem when his folks had gone to celebrate the Passover.

Maybe he stayed home to help Joseph in the carpentry business. Maybe he studied all those years, or maybe he helped in the community as a handyman. Whatever he did, when he finally asked John to baptize him, God sent him into the wilderness.

Jesus was in the wilderness for forty days after his baptism without any food. Toward the end of his time there, Satan visited Jesus. This was the time of the three temptations. Satan suggested that Jesus could make his own food from the stones, and Jesus told him that it takes more than food to really live.

Then Satan showed Jesus all the kingdoms of the world, offering them to Jesus if he would only worship Satan. Jesus refused, telling Satan that we are to worship only God. Finally, Satan took Jesus to the top of the temple, telling him to jump! No one will allow Jesus to even stub a toe! Jesus replied that we are not to tempt God, and Satan backed down.

During a Sunday school class, my mom once asked the question, "Do you suppose Jesus knew that he would only receive three temptations?" That's a question that isn't often asked, and yet I think it's a good one. If we knew what was coming in our future, it would be easy to hold fast to what we know is right. The problem is that we haven't a clue as to what our future holds.

We don't know if we should turn right or turn left. The path that goes north looks promising, and it may take us where we want to go, but there might be a chasm without a bridge, and we'd have to turn back. The path that goes south may be filled with weeds and thorns with a forest in the distance, but on the other side of the forest, may be a paved road leading to gates of gold.

It would be nice if all our troubles disappeared when we chose to worship God, but that is not the reality of the world. In this world we will have troubles, but don't be afraid because we won't have to face those troubles by ourselves. God promises to be with us—no matter how many temptations we face! We might as well enjoy the wilderness as best we can because we seem to spend a lot of time there!

Guilt Is a Heavy Burden

"Then I heard a loud voice saying in heaven, 'Now salvation and strength and the kingdom of our God, and the power of His Christ have come, for the accuser of our brethren, who accused them before our God day and night, has been cast down'" (Revelation 12:10).

In Romans 7: 15, Paul says that he ends up doing what he doesn't want to do and not doing what he wants to do. This seems to be a frequent theme in my life! I try to do the right thing only to have it explode in my face!

I was walking to class one rainy day and saw a skunk trying to move her babies out of a storm drain. Some of the babies had escaped and were waiting by the sidewalk, but some couldn't seem to get out. The mother was frantic! I went over, reached into the storm drain, and got the rest of the baby skunks out. Later, I was told that, because I didn't wear gloves, my scent was now on some of the babies, and the mother would probably reject them—causing them to have a slow, lingering, starvation death rather than a quick drowning death. What do you do with that?

Or the time I became so involved in reading a book that I forgot to do the dishes by the time Mom came home from a church meeting. It must be said in her defense that she had a lot going on that day, and the one thing she asked of me was to wash the day's dishes. She was so angry when she saw me sitting on the couch in the living room while all the dirty dishes waited in the sink in the kitchen that she brought in a backyard lounge chair and made me sit in it while she did the dishes by herself! It was awful!

To this day, a small voice in my head reminds me of these horrible deeds! It suggests that God shouldn't have anything to do with someone so undeserving of his love. I can't go back and fix either of these situations. I get embarrassed and want to hide my head when I think of them. I have asked for forgiveness many times over the years.

The nice thing about this verse is that it reminds me that it isn't God who is accusing me of killing baby skunks or adding burdens to Mom by not washing dishes that one day. God is the one who says, "It's OK. I fixed the problem. You are forgiven and forever loved!"

The more I learn to talk back to that small accusatory voice in my head and bring God into the conversation, the quieter that condemnation becomes, and I can move forward in my life—messing up other situations and asking forgiveness for new misdeeds.

God loves his children with an everlasting love. Isaiah 49:16 talks about God inscribing our names on the palms of his hands. You can't use an eraser to remove engravings! They are etched into God—like a tattoo! God has our names carved into his heart. He watches over and cares for us, the baby skunks in our lives, and even our moms!

Grace

"My grace is enough; it's all you need. My strength comes into its own in your weakness" (2 Corinthians 12:9).

(Author's note: This article was originally written in March 2020, but I find that it has implications for today as well. I think that times of national or personal panic will bring on similar reactions—whether the panic is caused by illness or violence or a change in routine, there is something about times of uncertainty that can cause many people to run around like chickens with their heads cut off.)

Have you ever felt like the winds of fortune are blowing you into the dusty, cigarette-choked, weed-filled corner of a cement monolith? Like you're in the bottom of a canyon of skyscrapers, late on a Sunday night, when everyone has gone home to their families, and you're left alone— by yourself—huddled in a threadbare coat, no hat, no gloves, sandals on your feet while the wind howls through the empty streets around you? Strange rustlings are in the shadows nearby, and no place seems safe.

There's something about this current time where things are spinning out of control! I can go to bed with the next day planned in my head, confident that I'll get everything done that needs to be done. The next morning, I wake up and discover that all the meetings that were on my calendar (meetings where a lot of energy was expended to make sure that I could attend) are now canceled. The new virus that is spreading around the world has reached a point where everyone is encouraged to stay home.

I understand why these precautions have been taken. I understand that the virus needs to stop spreading, and that the best way to stop its spread is to avoid contact with other people. What I didn't understand is how much I needed to be able to connect with other people!

My first response was to go to the grocery store, where there were bound to be people! I was right, there were a lot of people, most of them focused on the paper goods aisle or the refrigerated areas for milk, orange juice, and eggs. There was quite a crowd around the bread section, and some people were huddled around the chocolates.

While some people still smiled and said "Hello!" there was an air of desperation about all these people. They weren't enjoying the outing. They weren't gathered to be with people. They were on a big-game safari. Instead of hunting lions and tigers, they were on the hunt for toilet paper and hand sanitizers!

It's funny. I didn't need any groceries. I was there for vitamins and cat food. I just wanted to know that there were other people who were trying to make sense of this new world that confronts us daily.

What I'm finding is that when I need people to talk with, to validate my existence, if I just stand still and start talking, sometimes the monologue becomes a dialogue, and I find myself in conversation with someone that I believe to be God.

There are many definitions of "grace." One of them, according to the online Merriam-Webster dictionary, is "a charming or attractive trait or characteristic," as in "he possessed the saving grace of humor."

I have found that God can be both gracious and charming. He doesn't mind talking with me, and he has some particularly interesting ideas that I would never have thought of—if I hadn't taken the chance to talk with him instead of looking for more people. This might be a good time to "be still and know ... God!"

The Keys

"See these keys in my hand? They open and lock Death's doors, they open and lock Hell's gates" (Revelation 1:18).

(Author's note: This article was also written in March 2020 at the start of the COVID-19 pandemic in the United States. While people aren't dying on the same scale as they did back then, people are still dying and are still in distress for no apparent reasons. God still holds all the keys.)

John was communing with God on the island of Patmos one day, and he heard a voice and saw a vision of the Son of Man, who tells John not to be afraid. "I am First. I am Last. I'm Alive. I died, but I came to life, and my life is now forever."

This is the same one who holds the keys, and I believe that he holds *all* the keys. If you can open Death and Hell, you could surely be able to open the doors of Life, Joy, Comfort, and Security!

I saw a Facebook post the other day of a sermon given by Billy Graham before he died in 2018. He talked about how Habakkuk asked God what he (God) was doing! All this bad stuff was happening, and God didn't seem to care! Habakkuk had been praying and praying and crying out to God, and nothing was changing! Does this seem familiar today? We jump through every hoop we can think of to jump through. We use all the magic words, like "please" and "thank you"! Nothing seems to stop our lives from becoming increasingly narrower! We are shut down, and we can't find a way to open again!

In his sermon, Billy Graham said that God told Habakkuk that he would not reveal what he was up to. If God told Habakkuk what he was doing, Habakkuk wouldn't believe him. Graham said the same thing was going on in the world. If God told us what he was doing, we still wouldn't believe him.

I have no clue what God is up to. I've asked nicely, and I've thrown a temper tantrum, and he still hasn't revealed his plans to me. All he'll tell me is to watch and see what he does. I've told him that I've been watching him now for a month, and I can't see anything happening except that people are dying, and people are getting scared, and toilet paper is becoming as valuable as gold!

I have been thinking lately about bosses. When I taught, I would get irritated with my principals because they didn't understand what the teachers were up against—children who wouldn't listen and parents who didn't care. I then became a principal myself, and the view changed. Decisions had to be made regarding the building as a whole—not just for my classroom. Yes, I understood the problem of the individual teachers, but I had to think of the whole school, which included secretaries, janitors, day care providers, and food service personnel, as well as certified teachers.

I think that, when I look at this, I can see that God has a larger picture than just what I see. I still have no clue what he's doing, and I still check in occasionally, to see if he'll give me a hint. I trust, however, that he's doing something so complex and so widespread that, when he's done, we'll have to stand in amazement! I think that, since he holds the keys, he'll open the doors and let those who have gone before join with us in stunned awe! I'm thinking that will be party time!

Hang In There

"Hold fast what you have until I come" (Revelation 2:25 New King James Version).

(Author's note: This was written in March 2020 at the beginning of the COVID-19 pandemic. One can only live in a state of panic for so long, and then the adrenaline runs out, and we start to make accommodations to the situation so that we can have the illusion of stability again; however, we don't need to have a worldwide pandemic to have moments of panic in our lives. There are enough "slings and arrows" in daily living to warrant the desire for a day off.)

There is a poster of a black kitten hanging onto a knot at the end of a rope. The words say, "When you reach the end of your rope, hold on!" I have heard that all my life! Hold on, and it will be OK! I don't know about you, but I'm tired of holding on! I feel like I've been holding on to this rope forever now.

There is a song called "Just Be Held," written by Mark Hall, Matthew West, and Bernie Herms and performed by Casting Crowns. It says, "Hold it all together, everybody needs you strong. But life hits you out of nowhere and barely leaves you holding on." Sound familiar? It continues, "There's freedom in surrender. Lay it down and let it go! I'm on the throne, stop holding on and just be held."

It's so easy to get wrapped up in the struggle! New directives come out every day, and the numbers of people with confirmed coronavirus keep going up! We try to follow the rules, but what happens if you run out of milk, bread, or cat food and must go to the grocery store?

We laugh at the cartoons of mothers who are trying to work from home, and their children are shown tied up with duct tape on the floor. Or we chuckle at the father who, working as announcer for a TV station, is trying to read serious news items from his living room, while his boys are playing in the background. But the struggle is real! What do we do when the world is coming apart and we can't do anything about it?

We've been laid off so can't expect a paycheck. The kids are home for the duration, and we can't even take them to the park where they can run off their energy. The family still expects three meals a day and, for some reason, peanut butter and jelly grow old when that's your only meal!

This is when I remember Isaiah 49:16: "See, I have carved your name in the palm of my hand!" Do you ever stop to think about how big God's hands are? They would have to be huge to have all his children's names tattooed on his hands! He carved our names there by himself! He didn't go to a nationally acclaimed tattoo parlor to have it done with anesthetic. He engraved all our names by himself, on himself!

He's not going to remove our name just because we aren't big enough or strong enough or smart enough to figure out what's going on now! God holds us firmly in his hands. When we can't hold on to that slippery knot any longer, God invites us to let go of that rope, trust that he is in control, and rest.

That doesn't mean that we rush back to the lives we knew. I think those lives are over. It means that we aren't in charge anymore. God may not work things out the way we think they should go, but we're safer in his hands than in any other hands around! He'll carry us through whatever may come until Jesus comes in glory! It's the best form of multitasking!

What Does the Master Want?

"Don't live carelessly, unthinkingly. Make sure you understand what the Master wants" (Ephesians 5:17).

(Author's note: This was written during Easter season in the first year of the COVID-19 pandemic; however, these situations continue to pop up in daily life, and we can still learn a lot from them.)

It's been an interesting Easter, hasn't it? Not only are we missing out on the chance to dress up in our finest, flocking to churches where we can hear amazing music that fills our souls, but the weather has turned cold and bitter! What kind of Easter is this?

Actually, I think it's turning into an Easter that Jesus would be proud of! I've been putting my head down and pushing my way through this season of shutdowns—trying to remember things like "What day is it, again?", "What am I supposed to be doing today?", and "Is there something I need from the store so I can get out and see people—even if from a distance?" I was so proud of myself for taking care of myself and my household!

I had an interesting Saturday before Easter! I had two people call me, asking if I was OK and if I had time to chat for a while. I was really surprised! No one has asked me that before! I had a wonderful day talking with two ladies that I know and enjoy but who I don't especially run around with. It made me look at what I was doing in a different light! I was living carelessly and unthinkingly. When it comes to a choice between changing the filter in my furnace or talking to people who might be stuck in their homes, I think that it would be better to talk to the people. The filter can always be changed later!

I believe that we each have a calling. Some people are called to prophecy or healing, but I think that many more of us have been called to love others! Loving others can take many forms! It doesn't have to be cleaning their house for them, bringing them a meal, or mowing their yards. It can be calling them on the phone to just chat. Even if there is no disaster or great joy facing them, the gift of our time can be immeasurably precious!

One of the ladies who called said that every day she's been calling one person from the church and one person from a club she belongs to. What a great way to get to know the people that we see but never take the time to know!

If the body of Christ is the church, it doesn't seem likely that the church is a building! The body is made of the people of God. Some of us are lungs, some of us are kneecaps, some of us are pinkies, but we are all part of Christ's church. The person who is the left foot of the body of Christ might not live next door to the person who is the nose. The person who is the brain of the body of Christ might live at the end of the street, but if the "foot" stumbles, I bet the "brain" shakes its head and reaches down to help!

Something tells me that what the Master wants is for us to use this time wisely—getting to know one another and bringing his body closer together.

Who Do You Follow?

"That doesn't mean that Most High God lives in a building made by carpenters and masons. The Prophet Isaiah put it well when he wrote, 'Heaven is my throne room. I rest my feet on earth. So, what kind of house will you build me?' says God. 'Where I can get away and relax? It's already built, and I built it'" (Acts 7:48–50).

(Author's note: This was another article written during the first of the pandemic. One of the things that constantly surprises me is how often we try to create buildings or monuments to honor God. How often he must look at those offerings with the same love seen on our faces when our children bring us the gifts that they made. Nothing is more valuable than those rickety gifts made from straws or toothpicks and bits of paper glued together and given to us by small hands and hopeful faces. As this scripture suggests, however, God doesn't dwell in the edifices we create for him. He's the only one who can build something big enough to hold him—and he's already built it!)

This was an unexpectedly complicated piece. I was raised to follow the rules! You treat people with respect, give good value for your paycheck, and don't go more than five miles over the speed limit. When someone occupying a higher rung on the ladder decided that a pandemic was going on, more rules were added to the list.

It made sense, if a microorganism was causing a lot of people distress even unto death, and if that organism was spread from human to human, we should probably keep some space between all of us. When the order came through that we were to stay home as much as possible to slow the spread of this disease, it seemed reasonable.

Some people want to change the governor's shutdown order so that it doesn't include religious assemblies. There are some good arguments on both sides of this one. It could be argued that only allowing ten people to gather for a religious service is limiting our right to religious freedom. Some people say that God will watch out for those people who attend these services (although I've heard that after these services, the number of positive COVID-19 cases rises)! Some people say that people are more important than buildings, and we need to limit all gatherings to ten or less.

I guess this is a good time to go to an even higher rung in the "rules ladder." Joshua 24 talks about the time when the Israelites entered the promised land. They had begun to settle in, but they started to fracture. Some of the people began to follow the gods of the land instead of the God who had brought them out of slavery. Joshua gathered all the people and told them to choose which God to serve. "If you decide that it's a bad thing to worship God, then choose a god you'd rather serve—and do it today. As for me and my family, we'll worship God" (Joshua 24:15).

I believe in the God who created universes! I believe in the God for whom all things are possible, and I believe that God is more interested in people than in buildings. While the God I worship can't be contained in a building, if God tells you to worship in a specific building, I think that's what you should do. If God tells you to stay home, I think that's what you should do. I don't think that you can go any higher on the "rules ladder" than God! Just be sure that you're listening to God—and not to humans!

An Owner's Manual

"It turned out exactly the way they'd been told!" (Luke 2:20).

(Author's note: It doesn't matter if we're going through a pandemic or just living—it's hard when we don't know what we don't know!)

We've often heard the story of the shepherds when Jesus was born— how they were out in their fields, and an angel came to tell them of the birth of the Messiah, the Savior. How they would find him wrapped in a blanket, in a manger. The shepherds decided to check it out, and they found that the angel was right! Everything was exactly as the angel had said.

I bought a new lawn mower a few years back when my old one finally bit the dust. I brought the box home and carefully unpacked it. I unscrewed the screws it told me to unscrew, straightened the handle and fixed the pull cord just like the illustrations in the owner's manual. I was told to put oil in it—just to the max level on the oil stick; I was even told how to raise or lower the mower so I could have longer or shorter grass!

I followed the directions carefully and, when I pulled the cord, it started right up the first time. I was so proud—until I started cutting my first swathe of grass. I had black smoke pouring out of the motor and brown dust coming up from underneath. It turned out that I hadn't correctly seen the oil stick and ended up overfilling the oil tank. It also turned out that my mower was set so low, it was shaving the lawn instead of mowing it!

I'd like to have an "owner's manual" for this COVID-19 situation. Something that I could hold in my hands and look at and see what's supposed to be happening now—where I live. I'd like to be able to read that starting on May 4, no more infections will be occurring in Barton County. I'd like to be able to read that the businesses will start back up, people who were laid off will be brought back, and the economy might settle down.

It would be nice to have an "owner's manual" for people so that we would know how to explain ourselves to others. It would be nice to tell a joke in such a way that everyone understands the punch line. How about directions for explaining homework problems to the kids so that they understand quickly? Or even how to dress for this spring weather where it starts out beautifully and ends up cold and rainy?

Every time I fantasize about a tell-all book that would answer all my questions, I remember my lawn mower. It had a book answering all my questions. I just didn't ask it the right questions. The only one who knows exactly how things will go is God, and every time I ask him for a hint about what's really happening, he smiles quietly and tells me to sit back and watch. That's hard to do when I have so many great suggestions!

Muleheaded

"Staying with it—that's what God requires. Stay with it to the end. You won't be sorry" (Matthew 24:13).

Jesus says these words to his disciples when he's talking about future events. He says that everything is going to be falling apart, and yucky stuff will happen. There will be liars and cheats running around everywhere, but if you stay the course, you'll be OK.

Throughout the Bible—from the Old Testament and through the New—runs the idea of "finishing the job!" When God created the world, he didn't take a coffee break but kept going until the Sabbath, when he stood on his porch and looked out at his work. He took a deep breath and said, "It is good!"

When Adam names all of creation, we don't read that he named the first half of the alphabet during the first week and the second half of the alphabet during the second week. He named all the animals and vegetation, and then he joined God on the porch and possibly had the first cup of coffee!

In Revelation, Jesus says that he is the Alpha and the Omega, the First and the Last, the Beginning and the End. He isn't the A to K, L to P, and Q to Z. He starts, and he goes until he's done.

When the first inhabitants of North America came here, it is said, they came in waves from Asia, over the Bering Strait, down through North America, Central America, and all the way down to Tierra Del Fuego! When the Europeans came to the Atlantic coast of North America, they mostly came in waves as well. They all came to stay. It was too long and dangerous a journey to only come for a couple of weeks and then go home.

As people kept coming to North America, the East Coast became too crowded for some people, and they decided to go west. Some people went all the way to the West Coast before they stopped. The Western Expansion dropped people off all along the way. Some people settled along the Mississippi River, the High Plains, the deserts of western Texas and Oklahoma, Arizona, and New Mexico. Some traveled to the Rocky Mountains and the western coast. There was a place that called to all these people, and they came to stay. They stayed the course—even if they weren't sure what course they were on! They tended toward persistence—dare I say, they were stubborn. My dad used to call it muleheadedness!

We have a rich heritage of stubbornness. You don't last long unless you have a dollop of stubbornness in you. Those who don't have that dollop tend to move on down the road.

We haven't been promised an easy, uncomplicated life. Unexpected events happen all the time! Just when you are on your way to becoming a lawyer, you discover that you'd rather build houses. You have a good business owning an ice cream store, and you discover that your soul is wanting you to take up dentistry.

The question is which course do you stick with? Do you stay with your five-year plan, or do you follow where God is leading you? At the end of the day, I think you might want to consider God's course of action. As Jesus also says in Mark 8:36 (NKJV), "For what will it profit a man if he gains the whole world, and loses his own soul?"

Ask for Help

"Be prepared. You're up against far more than you can handle on your own. Take all the help you can get, every weapon God has issued, so that when it's all over but the shouting you'll still be on your feet" (Ephesians 6:13).

I have heard rumors that there are some people who have no problem in asking for help. If their days become too filled with "doing," they happily and readily ask for the help of others. If they are asked to do something that they don't know how to do or that they don't do well, they can delegate that out to others who enjoy doing it.

I'm trying to learn how to ask for help. For years, I lived under the impression that only children asked for help. Adults were supposed to handle anything that came our way   flood, fire, or famine, you put your head down and bully your way through it. It's possible that I am in a minority, but I don't think I'm unique. When I was growing up, the only time it was permissible to accept help was when you were doing the other person a favor. It was almost like we were to be pitied if we couldn't do everything by ourselves.

Some time ago, when I was teaching, I came up with an idea to have a quilt made for our grade school. Each class would create a square that we would then sew together. Everyone did a great job—until it was time to sew the squares together. I had no idea how to quilt and, instead of asking for help or turning it over to a quilter, I tried to sew it together on my own. It was a sad testament to how one person can diminish the impact of a great idea! They have since had the quilt done correctly, and it looks beautiful. I would like to say that I learned a lesson about asking for help, but it was several years later before I finally decided to stop doing everything myself.

If we're supposed to be prepared, and if we're in troubling times, this is when we need each other. We need to gather all our resources, discuss ways to make things happen, and share our experiences. This is when diversity is needed. We don't all have the same knowledge, and your knowledge will probably fill the gaping holes in my knowledge. I still don't know how to quilt.

We were created to live in community. This means asking for help—and accepting it when it's offered. The help may lengthen the time needed to do the task, but the lessons learned by everyone far outweigh the additional effort.

The time of isolation during the pandemic of 2020 has taught many of us the need for reaching out to others. We check on the elderly and those who are in fragile health, but I'm starting to think that we reach out to others because we need them as much as they need us.

The Reading of the Will

"Like a will that takes effect when someone dies, the new covenant was put into action at Jesus' death. His death marked the transition from the old plan to the new one, canceling the old obligations and accompanying sins, and summoning the heirs to receive the eternal inheritance that was promised them. He brought together God and his people in this new way" (Hebrews 9:16–17).

God is known as a God of Covenant. He makes promises that he guarantees. He hasn't made many covenants, but the ones he's made are ironclad. There's the covenant with Noah to not flood the earth anymore, with David that one of his descendants would rule the earth, and with Abraham that his descendants would be as the stars in the sky.

In the days of Moses, God sent down a list of rules to live by. God had done so much for his people, and he wanted them to prosper in the land he had given them. The first five books of the Old Testament make up the covenant of Moses. If God's people would follow his rules, they would do well and prosper.

The problem is that the people didn't follow the rules. In fact, humans tend to rebel against any rules—no matter who creates them. Half the time we don't even follow our own rules! To make matters worse, the religious leaders decided to amplify the rules given by God. Some of the leaders may have meant well, but the upshot is that no one could follow all the rules at the end of the day.

That's why Jesus was sent. He was the only one who could and would follow the rules. Because Jesus followed the rules, the Mosaic covenant was completed, and a new covenant could be set up. In Matthew 5:17, Jesus says that he did not come to abolish the law but to fulfill all the laws. The song "Glorious Day," by Casting Crowns, talks about this very thing: "Living, [Jesus] loved me. Dying, He saved me. Buried, He carried my sins far away."

When Jesus died on the cross, he covered all our sins so that we don't have to carry an impossible burden. When Jesus died, the old promise to Moses was put to rest, and a new promise was made. Micah 6:8, toward the end of the Old Testament, gives a good synopsis for the Good News covenant of Jesus Christ: Do justice, love mercy, and walk humbly with our God. If we recognize that Jesus is the one who exemplified this way of life and that through him we are introduced to God, we are promised eternal life in heaven.

You can't ask for a better deal than that. Not necessarily easy, but well worth the effort!

What Kind of Faith Can Heal?

"Faith in Jesus' name put this man, whose condition you know so well, on his feet—yes faith and nothing but faith put this man healed and whole right before your eyes" (Acts 3:16).

This verse comes from the time, not long after Pentecost, when Peter and John were going to the temple for prayer. A fellow who had been born lame was carried to the gate of the temple every day so that he could beg for money. He asked the two apostles if they had any extra money that they could give him, and Peter said, "Look at us! Do we look like we have extra money? But what I do have, I'll share with you." And Peter spoke over the man and removed the lameness. The people asked about this miracle, and Peter told them of Jesus and said that it was faith in Christ that healed the lame man.

My mom was diagnosed with leukemia and was told that she had choices as to her treatment. She could have radiation treatment and chemotherapy, and she might live six months. On the other hand, she could avoid the treatment and therapy and possibly live five months. She decided to just live her life as best she could with the cancer, and she died five months after her diagnosis.

It's one of those decisions that everyone must make for themselves— there is no right or wrong decision in these cases because there are too many variables that go into making that decision. Was she healed? It depends on your definition of healing.

I haven't been around many people while they were dying, but she had a good death. She had always maintained that God was her best friend, so why should she be scared to go to him. In the end, she just slipped away from us, and I believe that Jesus welcomed her home with him.

Maybe the faith that can heal is God's faith—God's faith in his son, Jesus, or Jesus's faith in God. I believe that God can heal people. I believe that there are people who have been gifted by God to "lay hands on" people so that they can be healed. But if we pray fervently for a healing, maybe using some special prayer with just the right inflections and posture, and expect God to listen to our petition, I think there is a danger of thinking that we are controlling God, and that never ends well. I think that it would be better to talk it over with God first to see what he wants to do.

Some hideous deaths can't be explained—babies left in overheated cars, car wrecks that take the lives of our loved ones, random shootings, or just being in the wrong place at the wrong time. No one has yet been able to explain the mind of God, and it's probably a good thing, or we'd probably use that knowledge for our own purposes. The only thing I know is that we are loved desperately and that we don't walk our paths through life by ourselves.

Sow Accordingly

"A stingy planter gets a stingy crop; a lavish planter gets a lavish crop" (2 Corinthians 9:6).

This seems self-explanatory. If you don't plant much, don't expect much (unless you're planting dandelions, in which case, expect a field to pop up shortly). If you plant a lot, you can expect a lush crop to come up for harvesting.

The problem comes when you consider all the variables in planting. Some plants require a lot of space to grow. Tree farms don't have as many plants as wheat farms. Tulip farms have different requirements from planting grass. Sometimes there's drought or floods—when you can plant 500,000 seeds, and they'll mostly die.

Here's something to think about: if your focus is to grow one plant and to grow it well, it would be better to just plant that one. Be aware, however, that if you want that one plant to grow well, it will take a lot more attention. You can be stingy with the planting but be lavish with the care. On the other hand, you can toss out bags of grass seed, but if you never water or fertilize, there won't be much grass to play on. You can be lavish with the planting but be stingy with the maintenance.

It might be worth rewording this scripture to: "Being stingy with your time gives you a meager result; being lavish with your time gives you a greater reward." Time is our greatest asset—more than money or talent. Given enough time, we can get more money and develop the talent (or be able to afford to hire the talent). Time is one thing that we can't control.

I like laying my day out early in the morning, determining what needs to be done during the next sixteen hours. When something throws a spanner in my day, it takes me some time to figure out what to do next.

It seems the world is full of "spanners" now. The weather doesn't cooperate with my plans to work in my yard, so I end up with a good crop of mosquitoes and grass that could be grazed by goats. My dryer develops an illness of some kind so that my clothes are just as wet when the dryer turns off as they are when the dryer started.

I'm learning to take a deep breath and, rather than mowing the whole yard in one fell swoop, to snatch moments during the day when I can mow a little. Maybe by the end of the week I will have mowed the whole yard, and my mosquito herd can be diminished! I'm learning that setting up drying racks throughout the house can increase my physical fitness as I do some "cross-country" walking around the clothes drying on the racks through my house! Rather than focusing on something I can't change, I can be lavish in sowing my time where it can do the most good. Life is a lot more fun now—even if it's a lot less organized.

Commissioned By Whom?

"My authority for writing to you does not come from any popular vote of the people, nor does it come through the appointment of some human higher-up. It comes directly from Jesus the Messiah, and God, the Father, who raised him from the dead. I'm God-commissioned" (Galatians 1:1).

I have to say that, for the most part, I'm leery of people who try to tell me what God is saying. Sometimes I think that people get in the routine of spouting things that they've heard without testing any of it. It's the same reason that many people thought the world was flat. They didn't travel very much, and all they knew was what was around them. The people who traveled a lot knew better, but it was a long time before anyone listened to them because "everyone knew that the world was flat."

We haven't changed much in some respects. We're told that religion ABC is the only religion. God set it up in the beginning, and it hasn't changed. I can agree that God probably set it up, but I don't know that he intended ABC to be the only denomination. There may be only one goal, but there are many paths to that goal.

And I would disagree firmly that ABC hasn't changed in the two thousand plus years since it started. If people are involved, systems (and religions) will change and evolve because the people involved don't stay the same. We build on our histories so that, even if the belief is the same, the process to work out that belief will be different.

It must be said that Paul wrote his letter to the Galatians early in his ministry and that many new converts, with their new commissions shining in their hearts, tend toward boasting. Give us a little bit of knowledge, and it's amazing how wise we become!

The part that impresses me is where Paul acknowledges that he speaks what God tells him to speak—despite everything. The Old Testament prophets did the same. When the high priest of Israel told Amos to go back home and stop preaching doom and disaster to Israel, Amos said that he never wanted to be a preacher. He was a farmer, but God said, "Go preach!"—so Amos went.

Many people, especially religious people, didn't like what Paul was saying. They had a nice little deal—only preaching to the Jews—and why fix it if it isn't broken! But God had shown Paul a larger picture, and Paul was bound to share that picture with everyone. If Paul had listened to the leaders of the time, we wouldn't be where we are now.

If you believe that God is telling you to share something, it's probably best if you share it; however, it's even better if you ask God to make sure that you don't share the wrong thing. If you ask God, frequently, to make sure that you are only sharing those things that he wants you to share, he will keep you from saying the wrong things. If, on the other hand, you start sharing things wrongly, God is quite capable of whacking you upside the head. It hurts to be whacked by God!

It Takes One to Know One

"Every time you criticize someone, you condemn yourself. It takes one to know one" (Romans 2:1).

It's interesting how different translations of the Bible will bring out different aspects of a scripture. We're familiar with the scripture in Matthew 7:1: Judge not lest ye be judged, but this Message translation of Romans, whacked me upside the head.

I hadn't thought about it in this light. It makes sense, though. You can tell a bad cook if you are a bad cook (otherwise, you might think that the food from their kitchen is gourmet!). You can recognize the behavior of a thief if you, yourself, have stolen. In the same way, it's easier to tell if you're a pompous windbag if I have also been an arrogant know-it-all.

So much judgment, blame, and censor are going on in the world today. Sometimes it seems like the only truthful, kind, and wise people in the world are myself and some of my friends. I know that can't be the case. I know that there are many truthful, kind, and wise people in the world. It's just that the other types of people are so much louder.

Having said that, I do have to admit that I sometimes shade the truth— but only for artistic effect. Sometimes I will see a loud argument going on that could lead to blows but instead of walking over to calm the people, I will turn and walk away because I don't need the drama, and, yes, there are many times when I am thicker than any of the redwoods in California and don't have a clue as to what's going on.

It's easy to say, "Judge not!" but we don't think about what those words reveal about ourselves. We'd like to think that we're far enough along the path of righteousness that we can help train those who are behind us on that path. It's not like the path to righteousness is like the path toward becoming a master plumber. Well, maybe it is.

Master plumbers or electricians or lawyers or doctors become masters because of the experiences they've gone through. They've failed in so many ways, dusted themselves off, and tried other solutions so that, theoretically, they don't have to think about the solutions when they see the problems. They know what to look for and if something reacts in an unusual way, they know how to pay special attention to it—to figure out why this is different from situations they've met in the past.

People who are masters of righteousness have also gone through experiences, and, theoretically, they've "been there, done that"—so many times they tend to spill out solutions without thinking. Master plumbers know that the first thing to do when working with water pipes is to shut off the water. Sometimes those who are masters of righteousness forget to turn off the water, and they keep trying to "fix" a situation while the water is still running. Lord, help me to remember to "shut off the water" before I drown someone in judgment!

Why Can't You Listen!

"Abraham replied, 'If they won't listen to Moses and the Prophets, they're not going to be convinced by someone who rises from the dead'" (Luke 16:31).

This is the last verse of the story of the rich man and Lazarus. Lazarus was a poor man, covered with sores, who was dumped on the front steps of a rich man's house. The rich man didn't pay any attention to Lazarus while all Lazarus wanted were scraps from the rich man's table.

Both guys died, but while Lazarus went directly up to Abraham in heaven, the rich man went to a place of torment. The rich man tried to get Abraham to help him out but was told that he had all his good stuff during his lifetime. Lazarus didn't, so it was time for Lazarus to shine now.

The rich man then asked for Lazarus to go tell his brothers about the consequences of their actions. Abraham responded with the scripture above. "I've already sent messengers. What makes you think that they'll listen to anyone else?"

I have to say that I have, at different times, been each of these people. I've been the poor fellow who is just trying to live his life the best that he can. I've been the rich fellow who is so focused on his goals that he doesn't pay any attention to the people around him. And I've been Abraham, trying to tell people that their goals aren't nearly as important as the people they trample.

I've come to believe that some people won't listen to good advice no matter what you do. They've read the books, and they've thought the problem out so they know the path they should take. I've been there! Even when someone who had walked that road gave me the benefit of their experience, I aggressively walked my own path—and got whacked upside the head for my pains!

Our culture promotes competition, and competition isn't necessarily a bad thing. There are many sports figures who are good examples of people who enjoy the competition of sports, but they don't focus on that as the total of their lives.

When we decide to set goals that we want to reach—developing a large bank account, becoming CEO before turning thirty, or even a goal of being married by the time you reach twenty—we have to be careful that we don't let that goal run our lives. We shouldn't be in such a rush to reach our goal that we lose the important people—not necessarily the people who might help us on our way to the goal but the people who will sustain us along the way and afterward.

Getting whacked in the head isn't the most fun way to learn a lesson. Some of us have been pretty beaten-up in the process of learning lessons. The problem is, after you've been beaten up by life, your goal is to help someone else avoid that lesson, but who will listen?

A Good Place to Be in Times of Trouble

"God is good, a hiding place in tough times. He recognizes and welcomes anyone looking for help, no matter how desperate the trouble" (Nahum 1:7).

(Author's note: The pandemic brought out many responses in people. Faith was increased in some people and in others, the faith almost disappeared. We still have times when we pray fervently to God for help in dealing with life issues. Sometimes we see quick responses to our prayers but sometimes, God doesn't even seem to be in the same building! Take heart! It could be worse!)

About forty years after Jonah came out of the belly of the whale to preach to Nineveh in the land of Assyria, the country reverted to its old ways and decided to invade Israel. Assyria was a ruthless nation, and God told Nahum to prophecy that Assyria would be handled, and it was. Assyria was conquered by Babylon and disappeared from the maps of the world.

God, however, has his own timing of rewards and punishments. Sometimes it seems like we're forgotten in the scheme of things. COVID hit our country like a tsunami in March, only eight months ago; but it feels like we have been living under the burden of it for several years.

We each have our ways of dealing with trouble. We become angry and fight back, or we withdraw and disappear inside ourselves. Some of us move away (if we can), or we run for Congress. These remedies all have their time and place. One remedy that merits a second look is taking our troubles to God.

There is a story about a fellow who, when he goes home after work, touches a tree by his front door. When asked why he did such a thing, he replied that he didn't want his family affected by his troubles from work. Before he goes into the house, he hangs his troubles on the tree, and when he goes to work the next day, there are fewer troubles to pick back up.

I know—it's easier said than done; but then nothing worth doing is easy at first. It has been said that if you can do something for twenty-one days, it will become a habit, and you won't even think about it because it has become automatic. If we can give our troubles to God at night (and leave them with him) for at least twenty-one days, I think it might be worth a try.

That doesn't mean that the troubles will go away immediately. I know many who have prayed for God to bring an end to this pandemic, and we still have it, but maybe, because they keep praying, it will end sooner.

I lived in Ohio for five years, and when I moved back home, I was talking with my dad about my time there. I told Dad that I had prayed daily that I be blessed mightily and that my territory be expanded to hold all my blessings. I told him that I had gone to Ohio poor, and I came home just about as poor. I suggested that my praying hadn't done much good. His response was, "Just think how bad off you'd be if you hadn't prayed!" It's certainly a thought!

I don't have a tree by my door, but I do have a stout bush!

Can I Help You?

"Accepting someone's help is as good as giving someone help. The smallest act of giving or receiving makes you a true apprentice. You won't lose out on a thing" (Matthew 10:40–42).

Unfortunately, our world seems to believe that while it's important to help others out, we shouldn't need any help ourselves. Granted, I wouldn't be of much help if your car is stuck in the mud (I'd be more likely to get my car stuck as well, and then we'd need twice as much help), but if you're needing encouragement to reach your goal or a listening ear, I'm good with that.

The thing is that there has never been a time when we could do everything ourselves. Whether you believe in creationism or the big bang theory, we've never been alone as long as we've been on this planet. We have always been surrounded by other lives—plants, animals, or humans. We've learned to work with, work against, manipulate, or coerce others to help us get where we wanted to go. That hasn't changed.

What is changing is our understanding of our interconnectedness with the life around us. If we aren't careful, all the help that we've taken for granted—the people who used to wait on us when we went shopping, the gas station attendants who filled our tanks and washed our windshields—will start to disappear. Unless we ask our students to help wipe down the chalkboards, why would they stay after school, and when would we have those conversations where we learn who they are becoming and how we can help them. Unless we ask our children to help us bake cookies or change the oil, how will they learn these skills, and how will we find the time to bond with them?

Creating a family is not automatically done through birthing children. Most everyone recognizes that some of the strongest ties are through the heart rather than through the blood. We build those connections one strand at a time through sharing the workload as well as relaxing together at the end of the day.

You can become remarkably close to another person very quickly when you're helping a cow deliver a calf or when you're helping to rescue a deer who has become stuck in the mud. When you're helping someone whose car has broken down, you quickly learn the concept of "team effort."

If we insist that we must sit on our thrones, dispensing help like a monarch granting favors to subjects, we'll miss the best part of life! When the monarch steps off the throne, the crown will probably leave the head, and a real person can emerge. Don't keep your "real person" tied up in the myth that you don't need help. Life invites us to drop our royal robes of privilege and to join the family of life that surrounds us if we but have eyes to see and ears to hear.

Fight, Flight, or Freeze

"Let the distress bring you to God, not drive you from him. The result was all gain, no loss. Distress that drives us to God does that. It turns us around. It gets us back in the way of salvation. We never regret that kind of pain. But those who let distress drive them away from God are full of regrets, end up on a deathbed of regrets" (2 Corinthians 7:9–10).

(Author's note: This was written in March 2021. Those of us who made it through the uncertainty and instability of the start of the pandemic and the attending violence weren't too sure where to turn. There was a thought that the disease was backing down a bit—not as many deaths were being reported, but then we heard that the deaths originally being reported as related to COVID were being misrepresented and might not have had much to do with reality. People were being killed, and while we first heard about the wonderful people who were being killed because of the color of their skin, it wasn't long before reports came out that these same people were drug dealers and not the law-abiding people we had first heard about. The economy was tanking and even the weather was becoming unpredictable. Where do we turn for help?)

This has been a season of too much distress! Illnesses, bad weather, finances, world news, local news, news from friends, family, and even news about our enemies are hitting us like stones thrown from a catapult. We can't see our people in nursing homes, but we can go to the stores. We can see some people but not always the people we want to see. We can talk with the people we want to see but only through barriers and not standing next to them.

It seems that, in times when we feel bombarded with distress, we have one of three reactions. We either come out swinging, trying to punch the person responsible for the distress, or we run away from the whole situation. The third option is to stand there, frozen in place, while our world collapses around us.

Oddly enough, the one that we most often see as responsible for our distress is God. How could God do this to us? How could he betray us like this? We've done most of the stuff he's asked of us! We're nice to small children and animals (kind of). OK, we did snarl at the old lady driving twenty miles per hour on the highway, but we were in the car behind her, and she never knew about it!

Here's something to think about. When we first become involved with distress, our reactions are usually knee-jerk—we don't even think before our fists are coming up for a punch, we're falling to the floor in a fetal position, or we're running for the nearest exit. After that first onslaught, however, a moment comes when we can take a breath. It isn't a long moment, but there is always a short space of time when we're standing there panting, wondering what just happened. This is a good time to turn to God.

We can be like Job and curse the day we were born because our lives are now torn apart. We can cry to God, asking him for an explanation of the sorrow that has taken over our lives. We can simply lie at his feet and sob our hearts out. Personally, I think that God is big enough to be able to handle anything we can throw at him. I believe that he sees our hearts. and he knows that anger or fear or sorrow will sometimes speak louder than faith. The important thing is that we are looking at him, and we don't stop looking at him. If we keep talking to him, he can fix whatever we're in. He may not get it fixed in the next fifteen minutes, but the circumstances will get better if we breathe deeply and give it all to God. If we walk away, we'll never know how the problem could have ended.

Growing Pains

"But how can I give up on you Ephraim? How can I turn you loose, Israel? How can I leave you to be ruined … I can't bear to even think such thoughts. My insides churn in protest" (Hosea 11:8).

In spring 1969, after I graduated from high school, I applied to Kansas State University and was admitted. Mom, Dad, my brother, and I were invited to visit the campus for an orientation, so we all loaded up in the car and headed toward Manhattan, Kansas.

While I stayed in one of the dorms, the family stayed in a motel in Manhattan. We all checked in with K-State and headed off for a weekend filled with learning. Throughout the day, I would meet up with my family, and I'd tell them of all the fun I was having. The odd thing is, each time I met up with my family, they would look grim, hurt, confused, and sad. When we headed home at the end of the second day, we discussed the weekend.

While I was hearing of all the fun that I'd be having, meeting nice people, and learning about my new place, my folks had been hearing about how they had spent their time trying to stuff me into a box of their making. They heard how the professors were going to have to work hard to open me up to the possibilities of the world. I was hearing about dorms, sororities, and fraternities, and the folks were hearing about Fort Riley and the problems with the soldiers during this season of the Vietnam War.

My time at K-State wasn't quite what any of us were led to expect. Traveling to a new city, continuing my learning about careers, and meeting new people didn't really change who I was. I was still the nerd who would rather read a book than go drinking in Aggieville. It turned out that no one had stuck me in a box of any kind. My folks had raised me to think for myself and to look hard before I made decisions.

God worked hard to raise the Israelites. Starting in Genesis, Adam's family was a hard family to keep together. Down through the ages, they would get a wild hair and take off on tangents—looking this way and that way for a god who would agree with them. Time and again, they would discover that the god they thought they had found couldn't give them what they needed. Time and again, they would come back to the One God, and he would welcome them home.

God is still welcoming us home. Every time we head off on our own, God takes a deep breath, knowing that it won't be long before we're at his back door, hat in hand, a little wiser and a lot more apologetic. There will come a time when we learn to trust God for everything, and no one will be happier than God when we reach that point.

How Did You Become You?

"By a prophet, the Lord brought Israel out of Egypt, and by a prophet he was preserved" (Hosea 12:13 NKJV).

There's an interesting bit of information about the people who left Egypt, led by Moses. We don't often think about it, but some Egyptians left along with the Israelites. Some Israelites decided to remain in Egypt.

We like to think that we are who we are because of the family who raised us or the part of the country where we lived when we were growing up, but that's not always the case. Even today, when we watch the TV footage of the race riots going on around the country, there are some white people who are fighting with black people against the police, and there are black police officers who are fighting beside the white police officers against the rioters.

In the final analysis, we decide who we want to be. We don't often realize that's what we're doing. We do what we do for all kinds of reasons, but I think it all boils down to doing what we think would be the right thing to do—and that can depend on the circumstances.

Teachers can face this a lot in a classroom. A student who is usually quiet and obedient can come to class snarling and belligerent one day. If we're having a bad day, our first response is to punish the student, but what if that child's pet dog just died? We get to choose if we want to be the kind of person who thinks first of punishment or the kind of person who thinks first of the child.

In the case of the Egyptians and the Israelites, did the individuals want to be the kind of people who had no regard for slaves, or did they want to be the kind of people who saw all people as worthy of consideration? Did the Israelites who stayed behind cherish their status over their humanity?

God brought the Israelites out of Egypt by sending Moses to lead them, and all who were drawn to Moses followed him out; it didn't matter if you were Israelite or Egyptian. Even today, we are drawn to certain people that we admire, and we try to act like them.

Here's a curiosity question for you: Have you stopped to think about the people who are drawn to you? There may be a group of people who want to be like you—maybe your children. Are you behaving like the kind of person you'd want to follow? People (especially our kids) learn by watching others. What are people learning when they watch you? We may have to start paying attention to how we behave in front of others. We might want to start thinking about why we do what we do, and it might not hurt to explain our actions sometimes. Compassion, mercy, and grace aren't always found where we expect them to be.

How Do We Know If It's Love?

"So this is my prayer: that your love will flourish and that you will not only love much but well. Learn to love appropriately" (Philippians 1:9).

When I was a little girl, I was too busy playing with my friends to pay much attention to the question of falling in love. When I was in high school, however, that question came to the front of my mind a lot. I asked everyone I knew—"How will I know when I fall in love?" Usually the answer was, "You'll know it when you see it." That answer didn't work too well for me.

There are a couple of items that I wish someone would invent soon. One is a button that we could attach to people's foreheads that would flash red when people were lying. The other is a button that we could attach somewhere that would flash green when we met our soul mate. Either of these inventions would be of great help.

Love can be a minefield. There isn't any easy answer to it. Studies have been done to define "love." Books have been written to help us determine the right clothing or behavior to attract "love"—books on how to "meet the love of your life in eight easy steps." They will tell you that you need to love yourself first, but how do we love ourselves?

If we love someone, does that mean that we give them everything they ask for? Interviews of thousands of people indicate that some of the saddest people have never had to work for anything. They are given all the material comforts they ask for but never have to learn how to deal with the realities of life.

Do we guard our loved ones, only allowing them to have joy and peace? And yet, how do we learn what peace is if we're never at war? How do we appreciate joy if we've never experienced sorrow?

Everyone is different, and everyone loves differently. The person I might think of as the perfect example of one who can't behave around others might be understood better by someone else. They might understand the reason for the uncomfortable behavior and know how to counteract it in such a way that this person transforms into one who can promote harmony among others.

Here's something to think about. If you find yourself with someone who has transformed from one who promotes harmony to one who creates chaos, it's possible that you were the cause of the transformation. If you caused the difficult behavior, it might be to everyone's benefit to walk away. It's likely that if you stay with this person, he or she will never meet someone who can release the pleasant behaviors, and the world will lose the benefits that it might have gained.

It has been said, "What God has joined together, let not man put asunder." The thing is, if God has joined us together, humans can't put us asunder. Sometimes, however, God wasn't really involved in the joining. It might be time to let him sort things out.

How Smart Are We?

"We sometimes tend to think we know all we need to know to answer these kinds of questions—but sometimes our humble hearts can help us more than our proud minds. We never really know enough until we recognize that God alone knows it all" (1 Corinthians 8:3).

This comment was made in Paul's letter to the Corinthians where he was talking about eating meat that had been offered to idols. Is it OK to eat it or not?

It's very tempting to look for one "correct" answer for most questions about behaviors. We tend to think in terms of black and white—either this is right or it's wrong—you either turn to the left or the right! But what happens when you need to go straight ahead? What happens if you're supposed to mow your yard on Saturdays, but it rains every Saturday for a month? Do you mow in the rain? What do you do if the situation is neither black nor white but sky blue or forest green?

So many people are crossbreeding animals now. I heard that there are few remaining pure bison now because so many of the wild bison have been crossbred with cattle. There are fewer rare cattle breeds now because people are crossbreeding cattle for different reasons, and some of the original breeds are being crossbred out of existence. These new breeds are neither black nor white but are somewhere in the middle.

There doesn't seem to be "one size fits all" in anything anymore. All the answers depend on the circumstances. One of the hard things about laws is that you can't legislate ethics or morality. You can't pass a law that requires you to be nice to others because no one can come up with a definition of "be nice."

We're not supposed to run a red light, but what if your wife is in labor, and your child is about to be born? Not many would stop and wait for the light to turn green before racing off to the hospital. It is illegal to steal food, but what are you supposed to do if your children are hungry, and you have nothing for them to eat?

Should we eat meat that has been dedicated to idols? It depends. Sometimes we need to eat the meat to show others that of itself the meat is neither good nor bad. Sometimes we need to leave the meat alone to show others that we disagree with their worship practices. Paul goes on to say that the only one who knows what we should do is God. I believe that if we ask God to direct our steps, to keep us on his path, He will do so. If we listen to the Spirit within us, it will lead us to the right choices every time. We can't do better than our best, but if we ask God to help us out, the consequences might not be so disastrous.

Moms

"She went ahead anyway, telling the servants, 'Whatever he tells you, do it'" (John 2:5).

Have you noticed that moms seem to think they know more than we do? The first dress I made using a pattern had a full skirt, zipped up the back, and was made with blue chiffon. Mom didn't particularly like that material for a beginning "seamstress," but while she rolled her eyes, she didn't say no, so we gave it a try. She was right. While it wasn't a total disaster, she spent quite a bit of time fixing it for me.

The first time I baked anything, I decided to try cinnamon rolls. You would have thought I would have learned something from my sewing experience, but apparently I didn't learn enough. There was a little more eye rolling, but Mom never said no, so we moved forward into one of the documented disasters in culinary history.

This scripture comes from the first miracle Jesus performed. He had gathered his disciples and was getting ready to take on the world, but before they could go too far, all of them were invited to a wedding in Cana. I can see Mary, the mother of Jesus, making sure that his robe was clean and pressed and that he had his good sandals shined to a fare-thee-well. Of course they were all going to the wedding. It would have been rude to miss it. Surely Jesus could postpone the saving of the world for one day so that they could attend this important event. So they went.

During the reception, the wine ran out. There was probably a miscommunication, and the shipping company had more wine scheduled to be delivered the next day, but Mary knew that someone would be highly embarrassed by this mess. Being a mom, she tells Jesus to do something. As a rational adult son, Jesus tells his mother that he can't do this. He's getting ready to explode on the scene, and to do anything premature would jeopardize the whole project. Being a typical mother, Mary looks at the servants and says, "Do what he tells you." At this point, everyone is looking toward Jesus for an answer, and the Son of God steps forward.

There are many actions that Jesus could have taken. Compared to saving the world, providing more wine for this wedding was a minor blip in the schedule, but Jesus took a deep breath and set to work to fix the situation with the result that this becomes one of the favorite miracles of the New Testament. It doesn't have anything to do with healing someone, casting out demons, or raising someone from the dead.

This is one of the best gifts that Jesus gives us. He pays attention to our lives. If something is important to us, it's important to him. His answers may not make sense to us, but in the long run, they'll get the job done.

Summer

If spring is the time of new birth, summer is the time of young adulthood. The time when we start applying the lessons we learned in our childhood to the realities of our wider world.

We move out of the family home and learn how to create our own home. We pay our own utility bills and discover why someone yelled when we left all the lights on overnight. We start paying taxes and learning about customer service—from both sides of the counter. We may have children and revisit our own childhood when our kids find their toes and discover ice cream.

Whether we have children or not, we learn that life will often have more than one "correct" answer, and the questions we were asked in school will often have great meaning for our lives.

All too soon, however, our lives start shifting once again. Our children move out on their own and have their own lives. Summer shifts into fall.

How Much Are You Worth?

Consider this. "What soldier at any time serves at his own expense? Who plants a vineyard and does not eat any of the fruit of it? Who tends a flock and does not partake of the milk of the flock?" (1 Corinthians 9:7 (Amplified Bible).

When I started preaching, back in 2008, I had a tough time accepting pay for preaching. I got so much out of the experience of standing with others and exploring what I discovered from scripture that it didn't seem right to ask for money on top of that.

Thank heavens, the treasurer of that congregation was very wise. He quoted 1 Timothy 5:18: "The Scripture says, 'Do not muzzle the ox while it is treading out the grain,' and 'The worker deserves his wages.'" After I clarified that he wasn't comparing me to the ox grinding the grain, Jim explained that scripture says that if you do the work, you should reap the reward.

We are taught that it is right to be humble and not to be conceited. The Bible tells us that when we go to a dinner reception, we're supposed to sit at the back of the room; that way, the host can come back and bring us to a higher place. Otherwise, if we plant ourselves at the head table, it will be embarrassing if the host asks us what we're doing there (Luke 14:7–11).

I have to say, however, I'm tired of thanking someone for their help and having them say, "I'm used to doing this kind of thing, so it doesn't really mean that much." I feel like I've been slapped in the face.

It seems to me that if we put in the effort—whether it's the effort to fix a leak, paint a picture, get a car running, or give a speech—we need to be gracious to those who appreciate us. It's like the girl who gets all fixed up, spending time to look good, and then when her fellow tells her how nice she looks, she goes on about "this old thing?" or how she just "threw herself together." It would be so nice if she just said, "Thank you."

Should we put a value on our effort? If we are employed by someone else, we can either accept their wages or leave the job. If we are creating something, however, we're using a piece of our soul in that creation—whether it's a field of wheat, a stone sculpture, a chocolate mousse, a great appearance, or a well-tuned car. How do we place a value on that?

I suppose if we're going to sell something in the marketplace, we should use the marketplace as a gauge for the value of our efforts, whether it's hard labor or the imaginative creations of our minds. We don't want to inflate our value, but we don't want to undercut it either!

I think, however, if we're wise, we'll remember the price that God put on us. We are immeasurably valuable in the eyes of God. If you put forth the effort, you should expect the acknowledgment—if not from people, then from God! Next time someone tells you that you did a good job, or your creation looks great, just say, "Thanks!"

We Don't Know What We Don't Know

"So, don't get ahead of the Master and jump to conclusions with your judgments before all the evidence is in. When He comes, He will bring out in the open and place in evidence all kinds of things we never even dreamed of—inner motives and purposes and prayers. Only then will any of us get to hear the 'Well Done!' of God" (1 Corinthians 4:5).

I had a meeting with fellow churchgoers at Mom's Bar and Grill in Seward, Kansas (population 41). I'd never been to Seward but looked it up on a map and figured, since Seward is so small, that there wouldn't be any problem in finding Mom's Bar and Grill.

I headed out in plenty of time and got to Seward without any problem; however, having solved the question of the location of the community, I had a problem finding my specific destination. A dirt road goes through the middle of Seward—Main Street. It has seven blocks on the west side of it. Since Mom's Bar and Grill is pretty popular locally, I figured that it would be on Main Street, so I drove north down all seven of those blocks. When I hit Eighth Street, I decided to turn east (right) and drove two blocks to a wheat field before turning around and trying the west side of town.

Those of you who have eaten at Mom's Bar and Grill in Seward know that it is on a dirt road, a couple of blocks west of Main. You must work hard to get lost in Seward, Kansas, but I managed to do it—all because I didn't know what I didn't know, and I didn't know a lot!

We jump to conclusions when we don't know what we don't know. When we are so puffed up with all our knowledge, it's easy to "get lost in Seward"! We do the same thing when it comes to working with people.

It used to be said of babies that they were smiling at people—until someone decided that it wasn't a smile; it was gas on their stomachs. We have all kinds of facial expressions that mean something different to different people.

I took a drama class for a few weeks one summer and discovered that the same expression can be used for mild irritation, deep thought, or going to the bathroom! Some people have mouths that naturally turn up at the ends so that it looks like they are always smiling. Sometimes those same people turn out to be serial killers!

It's a mark of great wisdom to understand that we don't know all things; and because we don't know all things, we can sometimes make great mistakes in judgment! That's just something to keep in mind the next time you want to judge someone harshly!

A Thing Worth Doing

"Don't fool yourself. Don't think that you can be wise by being up to date with the times. Be God's fool—that's the path to true wisdom. What the world calls smart, God calls stupid. It's written in Scripture, "He exposes the chicanery of the chic. The Master sees through the smoke screens of the know-it-alls" (1 Corinthians 3:18–20).

When I was a kid, people would gossip about stuff that happened at school or around town. This still goes on today! I discovered that if I really wanted to learn what was being said, all I had to do was to say, "I heard about that!" and stop talking. The others would then rush in to spill the beans on whatever they had heard. Whether or not I had heard about the rumor, by the time the others had stopped talking, I was fully up to speed on what was being said—not necessarily on what had happened but on what was being said.

There is a time in everyone's life where we want to be part of the crowd. We don't want to stand out. Standing out can be dangerous because you never know if people will think you're being brave or unaware. You don't know if they will accept you or throw you to the wolves. That's such a dangerous time for people. We find ourselves doing things that we may be ashamed of in the future—not necessarily dangerous things, but things that make us feel less than we want to be.

Some people never grow out of this phase. They may be lacking a sense of who they are, or they may be in the habit of defining themselves by the standards of others. They aren't living their own lives but lives that have been imposed upon them. That is a sad way to live!

I learned a valuable lesson in gossip-mongering when I was in eighth grade. I was repeating gossip to a popular kid in my class and didn't realize that the person I was talking about was sitting behind me. He made a noise, and I realized where I was and what I was doing. There was so much hurt in his eyes that I decided popularity wasn't worth hurting others. It's a decision that each of us must make for ourselves.

You gain a freedom when you decide to learn who you really are and to live that out. It may be the hardest thing you ever do, but it will be worth it! The people who came all the way out here to build new lives didn't take the easy road, and most of their descendants tend to avoid the easy routes as well. As they say, "A thing worth doing is worth doing well!"

I'm Getting There

"Yes, I'm on my way! I'll be there soon! I'm bringing my payroll with me. I'll pay all people in full for their life's work" (Revelation 22:12).

I have three cats, two of whom like to go outside. Those two go to the door and make this little squeak that only cats can make. They pretend to have a fatal disease that only going outside can cure. When I open the door, they rush outside. When they are ready to come back in, they'll either scratch at the door or they'll do that squeak thing again—this time pretending to be in dire circumstances that can only be fixed if they come inside.

They are not very patient cats, so they continue to scratch and squeak until I open the door for them. I have found that they manage the wait much better if I talk to them when I'm heading in their direction. Often, I will say, "I'm getting there, I'm getting there! I'm not getting there fast, but I'm on the way." I thought about that when I read this scripture.

Do you suppose that's one reason why God speaks to us so much? I know that I don't have the most patience in the world. I will ask God for something on Sunday, and I can give Him a week to either get it for me or to let me know why I'm not getting it. Sometimes, however, God takes more than a week to give me answers to my questions! Sometimes he takes years!

In the late 1990s, I prayed the Prayer of Jabez daily—a prayer based loosely on 1 Chronicles 4:10: "Dear God, please bless me mightily! Increase my territory to hold all my blessings! Please keep your hand firmly with me and keep evil far from me!" After a couple of years, I realized that I wasn't any richer than I had been before. I wasn't going without, but I wasn't becoming rich. Nothing much changed in my life during those years when I prayed that prayer.

I stopped praying the Prayer of Jabez. I mentioned to God that I hadn't received a flood of money, but I began to realize that I had been given gifts of equal or greater value. I was always able to pay my bills. I had been able to purchase a nice house that I really like. I had work that satisfied me, and I was happy.

Fifteen years after I stopped praying this prayer, I was in a fatal accident that wasn't fatal! I was riding in a car that failed to stop at a stoplight. When I looked out my passenger window, all I could see was the grill of a school bus! In a split second, the driver of my car sped up and swerved. The school bus swerved in the opposite direction, and we ended up with a dented rear bumper! Everyone involved was shaken, but after we had talked to the police, we were all able to wobble back home.

A week later I remembered those years of the Prayer of Jabez. God's hand was firmly with me after all these years, and he had kept evil far from me! Slowly but surely, He's on His way! That's something to think about!

And What a People We Are

"But you are a chosen generation, a royal priesthood, a holy nation. His own special people, that you may proclaim the praises of Him who called you out of darkness into His marvelous light, who once were not a people but are now the people of God, who had not obtained mercy but now have obtained mercy" (1 Peter 2:9–10 NKJV).

We have become such a guilt-ridden population over the years! It's a fact that, given a white sheet of paper with one black smudge, we tend to focus on the black smudge rather than see the field of pristine white! We work so hard to do the right thing and to be the right person that our focus can stray to our imperfections.

It has been said by many people that there's always room for improvement. That is true, but unless we take the time to look at the hard work we went through to reach today, it is easy to become discouraged.

Do you realize what you have accomplished? Just the act of breathing is amazing—ask those who are on oxygen or ventilators. Did you get out of bed? Another miracle to those who are bedfast. Do you have food, clothing, and shelter? You had to go somewhere and do something to get those. Very seldom do people drive around town with food, clothing, and tents looking for people to give them to.

Are you upset because you don't have transportation? Do you have legs that can carry you? Many people don't have legs and must crawl to get someplace. Some people can't even crawl but must remain where they are, depending on others to bring them something as simple as a bedpan or to change a diaper.

Do you have eyes to see the glories of this world, ears to hear the birds or the wind or the voice of a loved one? Do you have a nose to smell peonies or fresh baked bread? Do you have nerve endings in your skin to feel the soft fur of a puppy or the rough bark of a tree?

Do you feel alone in this world? Do you feel like no one cares about you, how you're feeling or how you're doing? Do you feel like no one would even notice if you died today? Here's the thing about this one—none of us have any idea of the effect we have on others! There are people that you don't even know who would be diminished if you weren't here!

Do you have plants or pets? Those plants and pets depend on you! It's all well and good to say that they are "just" plants or pets, but every living thing responds in some way to another living thing. Those plants and pets need you to provide nourishment and love. People may not admit it, but I will bet you dollars to doughnuts that they talk to their plants and pets. Have you tried talking to your plants and/or pets? It's amazing how they respond!

This world would be a poorer place if you weren't here! Whether you are a pessimist or an optimist, this world needs you! We are chosen for a reason! We provide hope to the world by our very existence! Just a thought!

Nobodies and Somebodies

"God deliberately chose men and women that the culture overlooks and exploits and abuses, chose these 'nobodies' to expose the hollow pretensions of the 'somebodies'" (1 Corinthians 1:28).

It seems that the world today is divided between somebodies and nobodies!

The somebodies are people who are rich or poor. It doesn't matter how much stuff they have—they recognize lots of people and lots of people recognize them!

The nobodies, on the other hand, are people who are rich or poor. It doesn't matter how much stuff they have—they recognize lots of people and lots of people recognize them (deeming them unworthy to be noticed)!

Do you notice something odd about the two paragraphs above? They are essentially the same! There really isn't much difference between somebodies and nobodies.

The somebodies like to talk more, maybe. They want to make sure that others see them and know that they are there, and sometimes they talk a lot but don't really hear what they are saying. They miss out on what's going on around them.

Nobodies don't say much, but they see a lot. Sometimes they want to remain hidden because they are more comfortable just living their lives quietly instead of being the center of attention. Things can happen when people pay attention to you.

Life can be complex. It's like the Mississippi River. Sometimes it rolls along lazily, following the same old streambed it's followed for years. Sometimes it rips through its banks and destroys people's lives. Nobodies are those people who focus on living their lives as best as they can. They know how to get what they need with the least amount of fuss, and they know how to manage their lives pretty well. That doesn't mean that they are in control of their lives (I don't think anyone is actually in control of his or her own life!) but it means that they know that there's a time to work furiously and a time to sit still. There's a time to enjoy your family and a time to be by yourself.

Somebodies seem to have no idea of the important things in life. They tend to be on display all the time, and if something needs to be done, they'll bring in someone else. If an activity doesn't bring them more of something, they don't want to do it. Sometimes I think that somebodies are nobodies in disguise, and they don't want anyone to look behind their masks.

If we're lucky, we can find a middle ground. We can be real! We can be ourselves! We can be a body! We don't have to be somebody, telling everyone who we are. We don't have to be a nobody, hiding away in a crowd, hoping that nobody sees us. We can live our lives in our own ways and not worry about what others think of us. If we know how to do something, we don't have a problem in leading others. If we don't know, we don't have a problem in asking.

Some people may call this straddling the fence. In most pictures of cowboys, usually one or two are straddling the fence. You can quickly get to either side—whichever side needs you the most. Seems to me that might be a strategic place to be!

Relationships

"All our praise is focused through Jesus on this incomparably wise God! Yes!" (Romans 16:27).

When I was growing up, we had family reunions every year. Grandpa came from a family with seven kids. Most of them had kids and several of those kids had kids. By the time my generation came along, lots of people at these reunions were from all over the state and even from some surrounding states!

Grandpa only had two children, and between those two kids, we accounted for nine of the cousins at these reunions. However, Aunt Winnie had six kids, and Aunt Jennie had seven! With all these people running around like zoo animals at feeding time, it was hard to know which kids belonged to which of the original family.

The thing that I discovered when looking back at this time is that while the original parents, Ida and J. L., were known as being stern and highly disciplined, their seven kids weren't all that stern or disciplined. Some of the "originals" had faces that settled easily into frowns and, since most of them were farmers, they tended to squint a lot from looking out into the sun. If you didn't know these people, they could be a little scary!

We had some cowboys and roughnecks, farmers and ranchers, as well as insurance salesmen, optometrists, and teachers—lots of teachers with those looks that could freeze students in their tracks from across the room! But when all the food was set out on those long picnic tables, someone was asked to say grace. Everyone stood up, hats came off bowed heads, and the food was blessed. That was something to see! All these big guys, standing quietly while some frail little woman decided who would say grace.

We tended to gather in our own family groupings to eat, and it was odd to watch a stern-looking grandparent with a toddler crawling all over him or to see the softness come over one of the implacable faces of an "original" when their great-grandchild talked about their new puppy. We got to know the "originals" by watching them with their kids and grandkids.

It's the same way with God and Jesus. God developed a strict reputation through the Old Testament. When Jesus came along, we were introduced to a different type of God—a God of grace and mercy who loved his children with a love that stretched to the ends of the universe, forget about to the moon and back.

We can get to know God through watching him with Jesus and how Jesus treats God. Because of Jesus, we can have the same relationship with God. We can talk of our hopes and dreams and know that God will carry these next to his heart! Not only that but he will share his wisdom with us!

He's teaching me how to cook baked spaghetti! We almost have it down pat!

God Chose You

"The next day he summoned his disciples; from them he selected twelve he designated as apostles: Simon (whom he named Peter), Andrew (his brother), James, John, Philip, Bartholomew, Matthew, Thomas, James (son of Alphaeus), Simon (called the Zealot), Judas (son of James), and Judas Iscariot (who betrayed him)" (Luke 6:14–16).

I happen to believe that God knows the end from the beginning. I believe that we have free choice in our lives, but I believe that God can see the past, present, and future all at the same time. He knows the choices that will face us, and he knows what we will choose to do. Believing this, I was astounded when I saw this scripture. There were three words that I had never noticed before, but they made a big difference to me.

Jesus chose his apostles. He took a hard look at all the people who had been following him—his disciples—and, out of that group, he chose twelve people who would become his inner circle. The people to whom he could open his heart and mind. The ones who would be able to understand why he did what he did.

One of those people he chose was Judas Iscariot, the one "who betrayed him"! If I believe that God knows the end from the beginning, then I must believe that God knew that Judas would betray him—when Judas was chosen as an apostle!

What an amazing thing for God to do! God saw something in Judas that was more important than the fact that Judas would betray him!

So often we become weighed down by the choices we make in our lives. The times when we turned left when we knew we should have turned right. The times when we turned our backs on our friends or our families. The times when we thought we were doing the right thing only to discover that we didn't have all the facts. The promises of justice that were never fulfilled, and we were left high and dry, swaying from the gallows we hung from.

We become convinced that we are worthless and unredeemable. We're like expired coupons that get thrown into the trash.

But if Jesus chose Judas Iscariot, the one who turned Jesus in for thirty pieces of silver, he also chose us! And if he chose us, he chose us despite what we were going to do. He chose us because he saw something in us that was more important than the choices we would make.

No one knows what happens to us when we die. People have given testimonies of what happened to them when they were declared physically dead, but that doesn't mean that these experiences are universal. A theory is that people who commit suicide will automatically go to a place of torment, but I haven't seen that in the scriptures.

John 14:2 does talk about the many rooms (or mansions) in the house of God. It is in my heart that if we were chosen by God, we have a room in that house, and we won't be evicted because of the choices we make.

As Paul says in 1 Corinthians 13:13: "There are three things that will endure—faith, hope, and love—and the greatest of these is love." Know that you are beloved of God, and nothing can interfere with that!

Thank You Anyway

"If there are corrections to be made or manners to be learned, God can handle that without your help" (Romans 14:4).

How many of us have tried to clean house or rake leaves with the "help" of little ones wanting to be a part of our lives? It isn't easy to rake all the leaves that have fallen from the ten sycamores in our yard that were planted to provide shade in the summer. Now that summer is over, and the leaves have fallen, we start to think that maybe we had gone a little overboard with the shade thing. The five-year-old comes running up wanting to help with the raking, and being a good parent, you point to a few leaves that you'd missed and ask your child to bring those over to the big pile.

The next thing you know, your child has run over to get the additional leaves and runs back to the big pile. At this point, in the time-honored tradition of children, the child leaps into the pile of leaves along with the four or five leaves that were brought over. The squeals of laughter bring out the Labrador retriever, and everyone joins in on a free-for-all that rescatters those leaves that you've been working on all morning!

Another good example is when your family is in church, and right in the middle of a long prayer by the minister, when the whole congregation is silent, your little one decides to tell you about the booger hanging out of the nose of the mayor's wife! This information is given in that "quiet voice" of children that could notify the next county about a coming tornado!

God tells us to come to him as little children, but we don't have these pictures in mind when we read that scripture! Instead, we picture ourselves coming to him when we are all cleaned up and listening to every word he utters. We tend to forget that children don't stay clean for very long, and their attention span is equally short!

The thing is that the King of the Universe can handle anything that comes along all by himself. That doesn't mean that he doesn't enjoy our comments on his work. I have frequently given him several suggestions on how a situation could be handled. They have been excellent suggestions that would have had excellent results. Usually God smiles kindly at me and goes about his business in his own way.

We can give him all the suggestions we want, and we can be eloquent in our proposals, but we need to let him do the "fixing." Sometimes his answers involve us, and sometimes he involves other people, but that should be his choice—not ours.

Every time I have tried to fix something myself to save God the time or effort to handle a situation, I end up like the child in the pile of leaves—scattering all the good to the four winds! God delights in my suggestions, but when I offer my help, he usually says, "I've got this covered, but thank you anyway!"

The Importance of a Good Storyteller

"No one has seen God at any time. The only begotten Son, who is in the bosom of the Father, He has declared Him" (John 1:18 NKJV).

The idea of a storyteller has taken a beating! Before the invention of writing, storytelling was the only way we could teach others what we had learned. If there had been no storytellers, there's no telling how many times the wheel would have needed to be invented!

Some people have a real gift of telling stories! As they talk, you can smell the grass and hear the breeze moving through the trees. Jesus was a great storyteller! With a few simple words, he could convey concepts that reached into hearts and changed the people who heard him. Pastors, preachers, and ministers ever since have tried to match the style of Jesus, but none of them have come close! While the Bible tells us that Moses saw the back of God the Father, no one had ever seen his face—until Jesus started telling his stories!

One of the things I've noticed about my favorite stories—not just biblical stories but popular stories—is how much I look like the hero of the story! It's amazing! It doesn't matter if the hero is 15 or 145. It doesn't matter if the hero is male or female, tall or short, fat or thin. It doesn't matter what the skin color is; in the best books, the hero always looks like me!

This is one of the hallmarks of the stories of Jesus. His stories don't have masses of people but individuals with distinct personality traits. We have the story of the prodigal son with three main characters: a father and his two sons. The story of the lost sheep has two main characters—the shepherd and a lost sheep. Both stories also have others involved in the backgrounds (the servants in the case of the prodigal son and the rest of the flock in the case of the lost sheep), but our attention is focused on the main characters. And at least one of those characters looks just like me. Unfortunately, I don't look much like the wise, loving father. I tend to take after the wandering sheep or one of the misbehaving sons.

These stories, however, give us a good look at God the Father! We can see how much we are loved when we hear how the father welcomes his erring children. We see how God can involve himself in our daily lives through the story of the birds of the air and the lilies of the field—how they are clothed and fed.

Lately, we've tended to look down on storytellers as tellers of lies, and some of them can be. But real storytellers tell truths that can become the foundation of our lives!

Love Is the Best

"But for right now, until that completeness, we have three things to do to lead us toward that consummation: Trust steadily in God, hope unswervingly, love extravagantly. And the best of the three is love" (1 Corinthians 13:13).

This is from the Message translation. Most of us are more familiar with, "And now these three remain: faith, hope, and love. But the greatest of these is love." We have heard Paul's definition of love so many times that sometimes we don't really hear it anymore!

Love never gives up! No matter what, love hangs in there! It doesn't matter what we do or don't do, love is available for us. It takes extraordinary love to do that! This isn't the kind of love that gives us a trinket or a special treat when we come back home or do something nice. This is the kind of love that tells us when we're behaving badly. It tells us "no" when we want to go our own way—and yet, when we come back tattered and torn with our dreams around our feet, forsaken by everyone we thought were our friends, this love gathers us together, enfolding us in arms that are strong yet gentle. We hear a voice whispered into our souls saying, "It will be OK. You are loved!"

Love doesn't force itself on others. God always allows us a choice. If he asks us to do something for him, we can always say no. The thing is, if we say no to what God is asking of us, we may be missing out on a great adventure! God will always have his way, but if we don't accept our part in that, we won't receive the blessing that comes from joining with him. Someone else will play that part, and they will get the blessing. Not because God is punishing us for saying no but because God loves all of us.

Love takes pleasure in the flowering of truth. Lies erode trust. Life is difficult enough without adding a lack of confidence to it. Sometimes we will shade the truth, trying to make someone else feel better. But how much "better" will they feel when they learn that we lied to them? I am a lousy cook, and I know it. When someone comes up and tells me what a fabulous meal I put together, I'm tempted to remind them that we are sitting in a restaurant! You can tell me that I choose good restaurants or that you have a good time when I'm around, but don't tell me that I'm a great cook.

It takes great strength to love someone!

Faith is trusting in God even if we must remind ourselves daily that God is in control, and he will bring us through this.

Hope is the belief that things will get better and that dissonance will be resolved despite what we see in front of us.

Love—true love—can't be contained. It's like eggs in quiche! It surrounds us and supports us and fixes us in the universe of God.

May love surround you and yours! May God whisper his love for you daily! Listen for it, and you'll hear it!

Generosity

"Be quick to give a meal to the hungry, a bed to the homeless—cheerfully. Be generous with the different things God gave you, passing them around so all get in on it: if words, let it be God's words; if help, let it be God's hearty help. That way, God's bright presence will be evident in everything through Jesus, and he'll get all the credit as the One mighty in everything—encores to the end of time. Oh, yes!" (1 Peter 4:9–11).

Generosity is one of those things that can only happen from a position of strength. We don't think about it much because we're always hearing about how if you have two coats, you need to give one up. If you only have two coats, it isn't too bad to give one up, but I have a feeling that we'd hold on all the tighter to our one remaining coat—particularly if it's cold!

It's easier to give something up if we believe that we'll be able to replace it easily. If I have a bag of chocolates, it's easier to give you a handful. If I only have a couple of chocolates left, I can share one with you, but I might not if you want both. It's interesting how this attitude is different between cultures. Some cultures don't think anything about inviting people in to share a meal while others are more closed in, only inviting close family and friends.

Giving a bed to the homeless? That is an extraordinary act of kindness. The world has become such a place of danger that very few would be willing to share their home—especially at night when we're sleeping. That takes a lot of trust in the people under our roofs. Maybe the beds that we give to the homeless don't have to be under our roofs! In that case, it would be a good idea to know where extra beds are located!

In addition to food and shelter, I believe that God gave each of us something special—whether it's a gift of gab or a talent for cooking, a great voice for singing or a deft hand at art. Whatever that gift is, it is one that we enjoy using. If we've been given a gift, we need to use it for the good of many—not just for ourselves.

People who are good gardeners can share their gardens with people who pass by. People who love singing can share their voices with choirs or concerts. If you have a love of creating art—whether on canvas or sculpture or clothing—share this gift with others.

It's like the saying about hiding your light under a bushel. Luke 11:33 says that lighted lamps need to be on stands so that they can be seen! In the same way, if you have an inner gift that you love, it needs to be shared. If the people you share it with don't appreciate it, it's their loss! Just don't be shy about the one who gave you the gift!

Any Day Now, Lord

"Every word I've spoken to you will come true on time—God's time" (Luke 1:20).

The story is told of the child who has a conversation with God about time and money. He asks God if it is true that in God's eyes, a thousand years is as a second. God agrees. The child ponders a bit and then asks God if it is true that a million dollars is as a penny in God's eyes. God confirms that this is also true. The child then asks God for a penny, to which God acknowledges that he would be glad to give the child a penny—in just a second. I think that anyone who has asked God for something has noticed that God's concept of time is different from ours.

In the late 1990s, the Prayer of Jabez became popular. Amid a long list of children of Adam, Noah, and Jacob, 1 Chronicles 4:10 mentions Jabez and his prayer. For a couple of years, I prayed this prayer daily on my way to work. "Please bless me mightily, God. Increase my territory to hold all my blessings! Please keep your hand firmly with me and keep evil far from me!"

I was offered a job in Ohio with a healthy raise in salary, and I accepted it. It didn't dawn on me until I was living in Ohio that their cost of living was also higher than Kansas. I kept praying daily until three years later when I realized that I didn't belong in Ohio. I came back home and was talking with my dad about this failed experiment.

"I don't understand," I wailed. "I prayed every day that my circumstances would improve, and I'm just as poor now as I was when I left Kansas!" Dad looked at me, smiled, and said, "Just think how bad off you'd be if you hadn't prayed!" That wasn't what I wanted to hear, but he made a good point.

God keeps every promise he's ever made. He just doesn't always keep the promise within the time frame I anticipate—nor does he always deliver the promise in the way I hoped for.

When I think of all the money that has gone through my hands, I am amazed at how much it adds up to. If I haven't kept it, I enjoyed the use of it. I don't live in a big house with a fancy car, but I don't think I'd like that. I have had lots of good stuff. I've traveled to amazing places, and I've met some fabulous people. I've read some great books and enjoyed the company of some wonderful friends. I still have my health, and, occasionally, my brain works just fine!

I guess, in the final analysis, it doesn't matter when the promise is kept. It's enough to know that we're not alone on our journey through life and that the answer is on the way!

Like an Atom

"Be energetic in your life of salvation, reverent and sensitive before God. That energy is God's energy, an energy deep within you, God himself willing and working at what will give him the most pleasure" (Philippians 2:12–13).

Scientists have decided that everything in the universe is created of atoms—tiny particles that can't be seen by the naked eye. The theory goes that atoms have a nucleus surrounded by at least one electron that flies around the nucleus so fast that they call it a cloud—no matter how many electrons there are!

The nucleus is made of protons and neutrons and is much bigger than flying electrons. The protons have a positive charge to them (like one end of a magnet); the neutrons don't have any charge at all (they're neutral like Switzerland), and the electrons have a negative charge to them (like the other end of that magnet). The image of the magnet is important in the understanding of the atom.

If the electron ever slowed down, it would smack up to the nucleus like magnets tend to do. The thing is that these electrons never slow down. They are like toddlers on steroids! They are constantly moving faster than the speed of light!

You are probably saying to yourself, "What does this have to do with being energetic in your life with God?" If everything in the universe is created of these atoms, we are also filled with atoms! We have billions of electrons rushing around inside us! Do you ever have days when you have so much energy that you want to go out and build houses or clean out your files? Some of that energy comes from those very atoms from which we are made.

I don't know if we are composed of millions of atoms, but it makes a good working model to explain a lot of the stuff that goes on in the world. Some atoms have more electrons than protons, so they have a negative field. Some atoms have more protons than electrons and so are more positive. They kind of react like people! Some people are neutral and can provide a good, stable foundation for those of us who tend to be positive or negative about everything!

I do know that the more energy I spend on being with God, talking with him and listening to his answers, the more I can see myself change in good ways. I have more patience with everything (except slow computers). If I see those atoms as God's energy working throughout me and my life, I can see an evolution within myself. It always starts with a willingness to seek God's will and to be open to his prompting.

Sometimes God's prompting makes sense—such as "don't take the cookies out of the oven before they're done!" Sometimes God's prompting makes no sense at all—such as "why don't you stop what you're doing, sit on your front porch, and watch the world go by?" Whatever God suggests will, in the long run, be much better for you!

Providing a Helping Hand

"You do so well in so many things—you trust God, you're articulate, you're insightful, you're passionate, you love us—now do your best in this too" (2 Corinthians 8:7).

(Author's note: This was written in June 2020 when the economy was shaky. We were trying to find ways for our local businesses to remain open while we were encouraging everyone to stay home. Our governments were starting to open their grant applications to keep money flowing into the economy, since tourism was highly discouraged. We were starting to hear about marginalized populations who were not receiving the help they desperately needed.)

Oddly enough, this chapter is about giving to the church. In this time of economic stress, our first inclination is to close in—to keep what we have because we may need it later. Not only that but there are so many areas that need our help. Do we give to help those in poverty? Do we help those with cancer? Do we donate to organizations that care for our children, or our elderly, or our marginalized? Do we send water to the Navahos to help them with COVID-19 or do we send special equipment to our local hospitals to help protect the people there?

The same thing was happening in Corinth. How do we deal with all this need in our world and how do we keep the promises we made back when we had plenty of money?

This is when it's important to pay attention to the words coming out of our mouths. Often, in the excitement of the moment, it's easy to declare that all we have is from God, and we want to give it all back to him. A week or two later, when mortgage payments are due or the car engine starts to leak, or we have a storm causing a lot of property damage, it is harder to fulfill our promise to give everything back to God. We tell ourselves that we need to pay our bills first and then, if anything is left, we can give that to God.

If we take a serious look at our lives, we can tell ourselves that God would want us to take care of ourselves so that we don't become a burden on others. There is sense to this, but do we really need all that we are getting? I love owning books. Something is deeply satisfying to me when I can reach out my hand and touch a book with ideas that I need to hear at just that moment. But libraries hold lots of books and, if they don't have the exact book I'm looking for at that moment, it doesn't take long for them to get it. I have learned that I can't say that I'm willing to give all that I have to God because it isn't true. I can, however, ask God to open my hand so that I can give what is needed.

We have been given so much. Even if we are not fabulously wealthy, we have people who will help us out. We have places where we can be fed and sheltered and clothed. We have libraries to help us think. We just need to keep on doing the best we can, listen to what we're saying, and trust in God to fill in the holes!

Who's Driving the Train?

"Calling the crowd to join his disciples, he said, 'Anyone who intends to come with me has to let me lead. You're not in the driver's seat; I am'" (Mark 8:34).

Have you ever taken a road trip with in-laws, young children (or teenagers), and maybe an animal or two? Everyone seems to have a great idea of where you should go and what you should do when you get there—or even what you should do on the way there. The result is a massive headache when you finally land at your destination.

I could never understand why my dad always needed to take a nap when we finally reached the motel. He always seemed to have migraine headaches the first day of every vacation. At least I couldn't understand it until I was in charge of a road trip.

I think this may be why so many people are addicted to checklists and schedules. If you have a checklist, you can remember to include everything you might need for a three-day stay far from the comforts of home—the Band Aids, the sunscreen, the tweezers, and extra batteries. If you have a schedule, everyone can be given a copy so that they all know to meet at the front door with their completed checklists and luggage—no later than eight in the morning so that you can get a good start on your vacation.

Has anyone actually managed to get the checklists and schedules to work? I can remember the tweezers and batteries but forget the cell phone. I could paper my kitchen with all the schedules I've prepared but somehow, while we may meet at the front door by eight, when we open the door, a relative is usually coming to visit us unexpectedly!

I was talking with a friend the other day and moaning how I wish I could follow a schedule clear through the day. She reminded me that my schedules have never really been followed. She's correct, but I'm also thinking that my schedules have changed. They used to have categories, like "breakfast, lunch, and supper" but not necessarily any times associated with them. My schedules now tend to list: "5:30 get out of bed, 6:00 have breakfast, 7:00 take nap, 8:00 get dressed …"

I've asked God about my schedules and why they aren't working any more. We had a good discussion about who should really be in charge of my days. Because I believe that God knows exactly what's going to happen during a day—what appliance will break down, which bill will arrive by mail, if it's going to be too rainy to mow—we agreed that he should probably be in charge of my schedules. I've asked if he could send me a copy of his daily schedule for me, but he just smiled. We're currently in negotiations, but I think he's winning.

How to Be Noticed in a Crowd

"Do you want to stand out? Then step down. Be a servant. If you puff yourself up, you'll get the wind knocked out of you. But if you're content to simply be yourself, your life will count for plenty" (Matthew 23:11–12).

At one point, I worked for a large corporation. I discovered, to my amazement, that if I wanted to stop someone from complaining in midsentence, all I had to do was to take responsibility for any errors I had made and to fix them. I worked with people from New York to Arizona and, when someone would call me to complain about how this didn't work right or that wasn't calculated correctly, I would say, "You're right! Let me look into it, and I'll call you back with a way to fix it." They would quiet down, and we'd end the call on a civil note.

People seem to shout their credentials from the rooftops, but I have noticed that the best coaches of sports teams will talk quietly to their teams. They will gather their people together in a huddle and speak softly. I think that this is not to keep team secrets but to ensure that their people are intently listening to what is being said. If you want to spread the word about something, speak softly, and people will listen. If you want to be heard, don't shout!

We seem to be in a world where everyone wants desperately to be heard—for whatever reason. People are making claims with no basis in truth but with a lot of "shock appeal." They don't seem to care what they say. It is like the adage "There is no such thing as bad publicity."

With everyone clamoring to be heard, the only way to be different is to stop trying to outshout the crowd. With everyone claiming to be the center of the universe, the best way to have them listen to you is to stop challenging them. We don't have to agree with them, but we can at least acknowledge what they are saying.

Another old saying is "Fake it 'til you make it." If you want to be noticed, be nice to others—and keep being nice. It's not that difficult to be nice for a few minutes, but it's much harder to be nice for long periods of time. We can be nice during the good times, but people will watch what you do when the going gets rough. If you can be nice during the long stretches of chaos and dismay, people will pay attention, and you'll stand out from the crowd.

The hope is that you'll develop habits of being nice, and you won't be nice because you want to be noticed but because you'll become nice. There are a few people out there who wake up each morning looking for ways to be cruel, but most people just want to make it through the day. If you help them, you will be remembered in a good way.

So, What Now?

"I've tried everything and nothing helps. I'm at the end of my rope. Is there no one who can do anything for me? Isn't that the real question? The answer, thank God, is that Jesus Christ can and does" (Romans 7:24–25).

(Author's note: This was written in August 2020. We were receiving directives from the federal and the state governments as well as many health organizations that contradicted each other. There was a time when we didn't know whom to believe, and so we tended to believe no one and to rely on our own wisdom. There are days, even now, when I'm tempted to rely on my own wisdom because of all the confusion spoken by the "experts." Hopefully, my wisdom says to check with God first!)

This is the tail end of Paul's famous speech: "I want to do what's right, but I don't do it. Instead, I do the very thing I hate." Paul talks about how, even though he knows the law, and he knows the law is good, he has a heck of a time obeying it. He knows that he shouldn't disobey God's laws, but he finds himself sliding into sin just like putting on a favorite shirt.

These two scriptures that end his confession fit perfectly at this time in the world, it seems to me. We wear masks to protect everyone and then we're told that "these masks" don't work as well as "those masks" and "those masks" are on back order, so go ahead and wear "these masks" because they're better than nothing. We're told that there are hundreds of people dying of COVID, and then we're told that the numbers aren't right because the reporting is messed up.

We're told to stay away from others but it's OK to go to the grocery stores and to buy online. But, to buy online, businesses must stay open to provide the products, and those people can't avoid their coworkers. Everyone became an essential worker—until lately when no one is an essential worker except medical personnel.

Businesses are failing—except for the businesses that are booming. Many people are out of jobs —except those people in certain industries. Schools were asked to stay closed until Labor Day, until the state legislature decided that they could start on an earlier date, and many schools chose a time halfway between the two.

We hear that this candidate or that candidate is lying through their teeth and no truth is to be found in them. Only our candidate is trustworthy, loyal, and true to the bone (much like a faithful dog).

I'm finding myself echoing Paul: "I'm at the end of my rope. Is there no one who can do anything for me?"

I've told some people that it's too bad that God didn't send operating instructions with us when we were born. Frequently I'm told that he did—it's called the Bible—and they're correct. The Bible gives us a lot of good criteria for making choices and decisions. It's a good idea to discuss things with God before signing your name on the dotted line. It's a smart idea to give all this confusion to him and ask him to sort it out. We can then move on with our lives without worrying about what we're going to do.

I'd still like to have something that tells me what to do when my knees don't work, or my brain cells start to leak out of my ears!

The Perfect Spa

"Are you tired? Worn out? Burned out on religion? Come to me. Get away with me and you'll recover your life" (Matthew 11:28–30).

(Author's note: This was written at the end of August 2020. Some of our prepandemic lives had become whirlwinds of meetings—whether business-related, family-related, or just gatherings of friends. Some of our lives were highly structured with little time to recharge our batteries. When the pandemic hit, many of us were running low on energy, so it was a relief to be told to stay home. Unfortunately, because we still needed to earn money to pay for our keep, ways were found to gather online or by conference calls. The result is that we became just as busy during the pandemic as we were prepandemic. At this point (semi-post-pandemic), instead of replacing some of those online meetings with in-person meetings, we're adding to an already full schedule with hybrid meetings. No wonder self-care is becoming a hot topic!)

This scripture is more familiar as the "Come unto me all ye who labor and are heavy-laden …" speech of Jesus. It is an appropriate scripture for our world today. Because of shutdowns and layoffs, staying home as much as possible and not being able to visit family in hospitals, senior living facilities, or schools, we have more time to get things done. I don't see, however, that we are any further ahead.

I wake up in the morning as tired as I was when I went to bed the night before. We don't take the time to care for ourselves. Jokes have been told about working from home in our pajama bottoms because we don't see people during the day. The Zoom meetings which have taken the place of office meetings only show us from the waist up so many of us don't care what we look like from the waist down.

Those of us who are not natural housekeepers are slacking off on more than our self-care. My carpets asked for my vacuum cleaner the other day. I remember my mom telling me that the mind takes on the same aspects as the environment in which we spend our days. I think that this explains the slow erosion of my thought processes.

We need to take time out of our daily lives to take minivacations. There used to be a commercial for soft water—"Calgon, take me away!" There was a lady in a bubble bath, sipping a cup of coffee with her eyes closed, and there was a suggestion that she was imagining herself in a luxurious cabin in the mountains or a beach house by blue, sparkling waters. She was taking the time to refresh herself.

I don't think that men are as excited about taking bubble baths, but they also need to take time out of their day to stop the frantic pace and to look at the world around them. This is such an amazing world in which we live. The days may have been hot and muggy, but the high humidity encourages the green in the world. Is there anything more restful than sitting in the shade of an elm or a sycamore, with a tall glass of something cool, watching the birds and the squirrels playing in the yard? Maybe a fishing pond would be more to your taste, with a cool breeze blowing across the water, and plenty of shade trees to lean against.

It doesn't cost anything to close our eyes and bring these scenes to our minds. In fact, taking a few minutes to refresh our minds and spirits can do wonders. In the Message, Romans 12:11 tells us to not burn out but to keep ourselves fueled and aflame. We're not very good to anyone (including ourselves) if we run out of gas!

Actions vs. Words

"They say they know God, but their actions speak louder than their words. They're real creeps, disobedient good-for-nothings" (Titus 1:16).

When Paul wrote this letter to Titus, he was asking Titus to set up the churches in Crete. Paul had introduced the gospel, and he was letting Titus develop the Christian communities. It has been said that it's easier to plant a seed than it is to nurture it through its development. So it was in Crete with Titus.

Titus was charged with finding people who would help him in his task. As it is today, when you ask for help, the first people who leap out of the woodwork are usually those with the biggest mouth and the smallest follow-through. Paul told Titus to beware of these people and to choose carefully the people allowed to help him.

I don't know why it is, but loud-mouthed braggarts are the first to offer their services for everything, and they have plenty of suggestions for how to accomplish anything. They don't hesitate to let you know that they've "done this very thing before, and this is how it's done," when, in fact, they don't have a clue as to what you are wanting to do.

If you want to know what people know, watch what they do. People who build houses don't brag about what they've built—they just pull out their portfolio. People who work in medicine don't make a big deal out of getting a splinter out of a knuckle—they just get the tweezers and start to work. Musicians and artists don't make big fusses; they just make music and art.

The more people talk about the fabulous things they've done, the more likely they are to have done nothing. The same holds true with things of God. It would be the height of folly for anyone to tell you the things you must do to follow God. God will reveal his plan for your life to you. You may be destined to travel around the world speaking to people of God, or you may be destined to raise a child who will ease lives of others. If we would spread the word of God, we need to live our lives in ways that show how we see God.

It has been said that actions speak louder than words. We can tell people how much we love our families, but if we speak of them in dismissive terms or loudly proclaim all their faults, how much do we really love them? We can tell people that we are great cooks, but if we have trouble boiling water, how likely are they to believe us?

If we want to build a church, we need to find people who want to learn more about God—those who want to draw closer to him—not the ones who only talk. We need to choose people with heart not the creeps or the good-for-nothings.

Faith

"We received the same promises as those people in the wilderness, but the promises didn't do them a bit of good because they didn't receive the promises with faith" (Hebrews 4:2).

Sometimes I have a problem with Christianity. We want God to do something for us, so we try to find the right words or the right gestures to convince him that he really needs to pay attention to what we're asking of him. The result is the unfortunate reduction of God to an ATM machine. Sometimes, however, we say the right words and make the right gestures, but the result isn't always the same. How do we deal with that? Is God suddenly against us? Have we committed some great sin that is now coming to haunt us? Will we ever be right with God again?

This scripture is from a passage that talks about the Israelites who were led out of slavery and ended up wandering around in the wilderness for forty years. The writer of Hebrews is saying that God gave a promise to these Israelites for peace and prosperity. He has given the followers of Jesus the same promise, but why did the Israelites not gain that peace and prosperity that they were promised? It must be that they did something wrong. They didn't have enough faith.

I believe that faith comes in many colors and shapes. It is not the same from one person to the next. If you consider that the Israelites had lived over four hundred years in slavery and were now being given the opportunity to leave that lifestyle, it would have taken extraordinary courage fueled by extraordinary faith to have followed Moses away from all they knew. And they followed him through forty years. Yes, they complained, and they moaned, and they whined all the way, but they followed.

A phrase I use a lot is, "bungee jumping of the soul." When I have said all the right words and done all the right things, and God still isn't giving me what I want, there comes a time when I must, metaphorically speaking, throw myself out into the void ahead of me and trust that God will catch me and show me the way I should be going. He has never failed me. I may have had to adjust my definition of peace and prosperity, but he has kept every promise he has made to me.

I made the mistake one day of telling God that it was more important to me that I follow his path for my life than for me to follow the script I had written. If he needed to knock me upside the head, I'd rather have that happen than for me to go merrily on my way down a path that would lead to no good. He has taken advantage of that offer from time to time. While it hurts for a moment, like the psalmist says, "Joy comes in the morning!"

Who Is the Real You?

"It's who you are, not what you say and do that counts. Your true being brims over into true words and deeds" (Luke 6:45).

One of the best things about God is that he knows us—inside and out. I believe that he created each of us according to specifications that only he knows. I take great comfort in that belief because sometimes I do the oddest things! I'm not always the sharpest tool in the box (as the saying goes) but, given enough times of falling flat on my face or being covered in the cream pie just thrown at me, I can learn. Many times I have been so focused on a goal that I don't see the people that I'm knocking out of my way to reach it. When I finally reach my goal and turn around for a victory lap, I have sometimes seen a path strewn with broken people, and I don't like that.

I believe that, inside each of us, God plants a picture of the person he sees when he looks at us. As we grow older, I believe that we unconsciously try to grow into that picture. Some of us may take a little longer but I think that's a goal that we each have. Some of us want to be smart, so we keep going to workshops or taking classes. Some of us have a creative gift that needs to be expressed, so we become amazing musicians or artists. Some of us can connect with people and become teachers or pastors or maybe even politicians.

If I could choose the type of person I would like to be, it would be someone who could bring comfort and joy to others—someone who could ease the pain that life sometimes brings. What I've discovered, however, is that I can say that loudly from the rooftops, but if I don't follow it up with my behaviors, it won't have any meaning.

This scripture is part of a sermon given by Jesus where he lists the Beatitudes and talks about trying to get the splinter out of our neighbor's eye when we have a log in our own eye. He's talking about how wormy apples don't come from a healthy tree, and good apples don't come from a diseased tree. I think that there's more in this scripture, however, than just what the words are saying because we've all known some "wormy" kids who have good, healthy families and some great kids who come from some pretty diseased families.

I think that Jesus is talking about God's picture of us, hidden inside. It's this picture that can provide a beacon for the type of life we long for. If we veer off the path leading us to be the person we were created to be, a red light starts blinking inside us, and we learn to back up and rethink our actions—because our actions reveal who we are.

If we say that we care about others but don't even see them when we walk past them, then we aren't very honest. If we say that we don't care what happens to others, and then we run back to give them our coat when it's cold outside, then we aren't honest, but at least we're on the right track.

Being Civilized

"The words that I speak to you aren't mere words. I don't just make them up on my own. The Father who resides in me crafts each word into a divine act" (John 14:10).

I read once that the first sign of civilization was a skeleton found with a broken leg that had been mended. The anthropologist who made the statement said that this leg hadn't healed on its own—it had been set, and the person had been tended until the leg was good again. Someone had set that broken leg for the person. Someone had taken care of the owner of the broken leg until everything was working again. Someone had "brought over a casserole," and someone had "cleaned house" until everything was back to normal.

Isn't this what we're supposed to do for others? If someone needs help that we can provide, shouldn't we at least try to provide that help? Granted, sometimes the "help" I provide isn't always the "help" that's needed—like the cartoon of the Boy Scout helping the old lady cross the street when her destination was just next door.

I'm not very good with tools. I'm more likely to hit my thumb with the hammer than I am to hit the nail, and what I know about plumbing wouldn't even fill a thimble. I'm not bad with words, though. I sure know a lot of them, and somewhere in that mass of words, there should be some that could help. Sometimes I even manage to say the "right" words.

Words are just noises that have been given meaning. Sometimes those sounds are overused or are used in ways that don't make sense, so they become meaningless; but sometimes, out of a meaningless clutter of words, something will stand out. Sometimes it's just a phrase or a thought that catches our ear and gives us something else to think about. Sometimes it's just the fact that someone is standing with us in the muck and mire of daily life so that we're not alone.

If our goal is to help others, I believe that God will provide the words and the actions that are needed. What we need isn't always what we want. I may want just a cup of sugar to make cookies, but if I'm feeling overwhelmed, what I need are the cookies already made!

If you've broken your leg and can't get around, call someone. You might make a new friend. If you feel an urge to call someone, do it. You may be their answer to prayer.

Blowing in the Wind

"Totally exasperated, Paul had finally had it with them and gave it up as a bad job. 'Have it your way, then,' he said. 'You've made your bed, now lie in it. From now on I'm spending my time with the other nations'" (Acts 18:6).

At the beginning of Paul's ministry, after his adventures in Damascus, he preached to both Jews and Gentiles, starting in the synagogues. When he came to Corinth, however, he was compelled to announce to the Jews that Jesus was the Christ—the Son of God. The Jews were not happy to hear this and tried to silence him, but Paul was not one who was easily silenced. He became angry, threw up his hands, and walked away.

Many of us tend to hammer at something until it's fixed. If we're good with hammers, this wouldn't be a bad idea; but some of us tend to hit our own thumbs instead of the wood. For those of us who have problems with hammers, it would be better to follow Paul's example. Nothing good can come if my hard head meets up with your hard head. I think that we would both dig in our heels and upset the whole community!

The good thing is that God has this covered. As soon as Paul walked away, he went to stay with a family who lived next door to the synagogue and who believed what he preached. Because of his new location, Paul was able to speak with the Jews individually, and several of them converted to Christianity.

It's tempting to think that we know how everyone should live their lives. It's much easier for me to see the wrong choices you've made with your life. I would be glad to let you know the error of your ways, but I have a feeling that you would come back to let me know the error of my ways. It could get kind of messy!

I believe that we have each received a gift from God that allows us to connect to certain people. Some of us are designed to work well with "opinionated" people, and some of us are designed to work well with those seeking to learn truth wherever it may be found. Some have a connection with people who have a great sense of style while others work better with those who have no concern with outer appearance (sometimes known as "slobs"). We each need to find the people with whom we feel comfortable.

It isn't that we don't like many different types of people but, if we're going to do some serious ministry, we need to find the people who will listen—like Paul did. Otherwise, our words will not find fertile ground in someone's soul but will end up blowing away in the air like so many dandelion seeds. Do what you love to do where you love to do it. God is love! He'll set you up exactly where you need to be.

Speak Softly and Carry a Big Stick

"It's true that moral guidance and counsel need to be given, but the way you say it and to whom you say it are as important as what you say" (1 Timothy 1:8).

Everyone is different, and we can each hear the same words differently. When I was a little girl growing up, I'd ask Dad's advice. Do I have to go to the birthday party? Why do I have to eat my brussels sprouts? Usually he would tell me, "Do what you want to do!" The only time I got another answer was when I told him that I had been asked by a fellow to join him in his treehouse by the river to study for an English test. The answer Dad gave me was no!

It took me a long time to discover that I needed to frame my question differently. Instead of asking what I should do, I should have been asking, "What would you do, Dad, in this situation?" I got much better answers when I reworded the questions. Dad would tell me why he would take these actions so I could use the same advice in different circumstances.

Sometimes we see people who are heading toward a slippery slope that we have been down and have fought hard to claw our way back up again. In our panic to save them, we may start out by yelling and waving our arms around. Some people will respond positively and do what you ask, but some people will only run faster toward the danger (or run quickly away from you).

There are so many possible situations in life. We don't only play the odds in horse races. The probability of being struck by lightning when you step out of the door goes up if it's raining and you happen to be flying a kite with a metal key tied to the kite's tail. One person can't possibly have experience of every situation.

That's why it's important to pay attention when someone starts talking about things they've gone through. It's even better if we know the person talking. If it's someone who sees ghosts behind every door, we might be a little skeptical when they start talking about seeing more ghosts. If it's someone who doesn't usually say much, but now they're looking right at you and telling you of what they've been through, we probably should pay more attention.

People often say that Teddy Roosevelt was the first to say, "Speak softly and carry a big stick." I looked it up, and it seems that no one really knows where it came from. Roosevelt claimed it was a West African saying. It isn't a bad approach to just about everything. People are more likely to listen if we speak softly. If we just happen to have a big stick behind our backs that stands up over our heads, it can only add to the intimidation factor.

Fall

Fall is the time when we realize that we have a wealth of knowledge gained through years of living—that no one seems to want! We start to become more aware of our health (mostly because it's starting to fail).

We're not as focused on earning a living and are becoming more focused on learning about ourselves and what we love to do. Rather than being forced to go to school, many of us find ourselves joyfully checking out college courses or workshops. We dance out the door to learn about pottery or tai chi. In a way, we are learning and exploring our worlds in much the same way we did in childhood.

In fall, we become more aware of the passage of time. We learn to work smarter because we're starting to slow down, and our muscles and joints don't work as well as they used to. We find ourselves enjoying the world around us—traveling or just sitting in the back yard with a cup of coffee watching the sun set.

All too soon, however, the seasons start to change again. The leaves fall from the trees, and the weather becomes colder. Fall is evolving into winter.

Strangers and Angels

"Do not forget to entertain strangers, for by so doing some have unwittingly entertained angels" (Hebrews 13:2 NKJV).

I saw a video on Facebook that was supposedly taken by a security camera that was motion activated. You can see it scanning the yards across the street, and then it turns to inside the house, and you see the huge nose of a German shepherd. The dog is watching the camera (trying to discover if it is friend or foe), and the camera is watching the dog (recording activity in case it is needed to convict of a burglary)!

How can we tell if the poorly dressed stranger sitting beside a stalled car needs help or is trying to pull a scam? By the same token, I read about a couple who set up an account for a homeless person, asking others for money. When a lot of money had been collected, the couple walked off with it—leaving the homeless person just as poor as before!

We want to help other people. It makes us feel good to think that we could be able to help others, especially if we have been helped before. If we have needed a lot of help in the past, it's easy for us to feel diminished—as if we aren't enough somehow. If we can find a way to help someone else, we feel enlarged. We have enough for ourselves *and* someone else!

How can we help others and stay safe? How can we help others without being taken for a fool?

I think that these are questions that everyone must answer for themselves. It's one thing to help young children purchase small gifts for family members. It's another thing to invite a stranger into your car! It also makes a difference if you know the person you're trying to help.

The thing is that Jesus helped everyone. When he healed the ten lepers, he didn't ask them for financial statements or references. He just healed them. The sad thing is that only one out of the ten took the time to thank him. That didn't stop Jesus. He healed lots of people!

That is one side of the balance. The other side is that Jesus is also God. I have a feeling that, if a stranger had asked for a ride, Jesus would have given him one. If the stranger then pulled out a baseball bat to knock Jesus out and steal the car, Jesus could have zapped him! Jesus has a lot more tricks up his sleeve than we do.

It can be argued that since Jesus lives in us, we have access to his tricks. The question then becomes, how fully do we trust Jesus to protect us from others? This is probably the foundational question we need to answer for ourselves, and the answer is probably different from one person to the next.

The great thing is that, due to the grace of God, he takes each of us where and as we are, and he loves us anyway!

If All Else Fails, Be Kind

"Summing up: be agreeable, be sympathetic, be loving, be compassionate, be humble. That goes for all of you, no exceptions. No retaliation. No sharp-tongued sarcasm. Instead, bless; that's your job, to bless. You'll be a blessing and get a blessing" (1 Peter 3:8–9).

There are moments in our lives where everything goes right. We get up in the morning, and our day just flows like champagne with sparkles and joy that last until late into the evening and, when we lie our heads on our pillows at night, we do so with a smile on our faces and peace in our hearts.

Sometimes, however, there are days of tension and warfare and enmity among the people around us. Sometimes we shout and argue and raise our fists. We can become so caught up in the anger that we don't even pay any attention to the people around us! We only listen to the words that inflame us.

I used to work for a pension administration company, and I learned early in my career that when someone called me to tell me about an error that had occurred, they would be disarmed when I apologized up front and took responsibility for my actions. People are used to hearing excuses when mistakes are made. They aren't too sure what to do when a person accepts responsibility. Usually, when they hear that I'm claiming responsibility, we can start talking together. We dialogue with each other—listening to each other and working together to find a solution that meets all (or most) of the needs of everyone.

There are many tricks on how to turn away wrath with a softly spoken word. Sometimes, all we must do is sit quietly while the other person empties themselves of the poisons within them. Mostly the tricks have to do with teaching yourself to keep from throwing gasoline on the fire!

There are times when the proper response to a situation seems to be punching someone in the nose! There is a popular phrase from the musical *Fiddler on the Roof*. The main character is quoting from the Old Testament: "An eye for an eye and a tooth for a tooth." He comments that we'll all be blind and toothless! If you really want to exact revenge on someone, it's best to leave that to God. He knows exactly how to avenge His children!

What we can do when someone is trying to disrupt a situation is to break the cycle. If they are itching for a fight, don't give it to them. If they are looking for a resolution, help them find it. If they are looking for peace and grace, help provide it.

Here's something that we generally don't pay attention to: You can't give to others that which you do not have yourself! You can't help a person find resolution to a situation if you don't have curiosity and empathy within yourself. You can't give grace and peace to others if you don't have it yourself!

Sometimes the best response to a difficult situation is to remove yourself from it!

Peace be unto you and your household!

Peace

"May the Master of Peace himself give you the gift of getting along with each other at all times, in all ways. May the Master be truly among you!" (2 Thessalonians 3:16).

Peace is what we want to find at the end of a long, confusing, hectic day! Peace is what we look for after a night of pacing the floor with a colicky baby or waiting up for a teenager out past curfew. Peace is what we want after working with long lines of customers who are angry because they must wait a minute or two for the computers to complete their processing.

Peace is what we expect when we stand on a sandy beach watching the ocean tides sending roll after roll of water sliding onto the beach after traveling halfway around the world. Peace is what we expect to find when we stand on a mountaintop and look to the horizon, seeing valleys and mountains all around us, or when we walk in a forest and see the deer standing and watching us.

It seems that the world is becoming more chaotic by the minute, and we are expected to be the island of calm amid the chaos! Who can maintain that pose for over fifteen minutes (if that long)?

Many people have found peace at spas! For an amount of money, you can slide into perfumed whirlpools and feel your tension fade away. You can lie on a table and have magic fingers massage away those knots in your shoulders and back. You can smell scented air and breathe deeply of aromatic oils that will do away with your stress.

What if you don't have the money to go somewhere else to find peace? What do you do if your children are screaming, your boss is angry, and the soup boiled over on the stove?

I remember hearing once that if you move away because you don't like your neighbors, you are likely to not like any new neighbors you end up with. The idea is that if we are creating our own chaos, we'll take that chaos with us wherever we go. Peace is a lot like that chaos. If we can create the one, we can create the other.

I would bet a whole nickel that there are families who live on the beach or in the mountains who also long for peace. Many of the people who work in spas long for peace. How do they find their peace?

I think peace can be carried with you wherever you go. There is a reason why so many people advise us to close our eyes and count slowly to ten (or possibly one hundred, if you can get away with it) before doing anything. We count our breaths. We unplug our technology.

It's easier to turn off our cell phones than to turn off the people who are around us. It's possible that this is the real reason why there are those locks on the inside of the toilets in public restrooms—or why bathrooms so often have locks.

Washed in God's Love

"It wasn't so long ago that we ourselves were stupid and stubborn, dupes of sin, ordered every which way by our glands, going around with a chip on our shoulder, hated and hating back. But when God, our kind and loving Savior God, stepped in, he saved us from all that. It was all his doing; we had nothing to do with it. He gave us a good bath, and we came out new people, washed inside and out by the Holy Spirit" (Titus 3:3–6).

One of the worst visuals in Christianity is the phrase "washed by the blood"! Somehow, when I hear that phrase, I see a vision of the trailer for the horror film *Carrie* that came out in 1976. I never watched the movie (I'm not good with horror films), but I remember seeing the part where Carrie is at her high school prom and is dowsed with blood on the dance floor. As I understand it, she unleashes her telekinetic powers and sets the school on fire (a bit extreme but totally understandable).

Blood is sticky and slimy and hard to remove from clothes. The idea of being washed in blood is not appetizing. In fact, this is part of why the earliest Christians were labeled as cannibals—we ate the body of our Lord and drank his blood.

Starting in Exodus and continuing in Deuteronomy, the Old Testament talks about justice. An eye for an eye and a tooth for a tooth—all the way up to a life for a life. If you take someone's life, your life should then be forfeited.

God sent down ten commandments that we were all to follow. To "make things easier" for the average person to understand, those ten laws were developed into 613 laws outlining the things we were supposed to do and the things we weren't supposed to do.

There was no way anyone could obey all those laws, and the belief was that if you broke one law, you were determined to have broken all the laws. This is why the idea of sacrifice was started. If you couldn't obey all the laws, you would give a life for a life. You could trade the life of your lamb, or goat, or dove for your life, and you would be forgiven of your sins and could then be able to sit in the company of God.

Thank heavens, Jesus came along. The New Testament talks about the sacrifice that Jesus made for us. We don't have to kill our livestock to be able to sit with God. When Jesus died on the cross, he sacrificed himself for us out of love. Now we drink grape juice or wine and eat bread to remind ourselves of his sacrifice.

This doesn't diminish the size of the sacrifice. If we take a balance scale and put God on one side, the only way we could sit in his presence would be for an equally enormous presence to join us on our side of the scale. With the sacrifice of Jesus, the Son of God, we have that presence joining us.

All we must do is invite Jesus to sit with us, and he's right there. We don't have to bathe in blood to sit with God; we've been washed in his love!

The Strong Man

"Those of us who are strong and able in the faith need to step in and lend a hand to those who falter, and not just do what is most convenient for us. Strength is for service, not status" (Romans 15:1).

I am basically a cave dweller in that my favorite place to be is on my couch, reading a good book, listening to good music, and possibly eating chocolate. The sad thing is that you can't make a lot of money doing this! Not only that, but it is extremely hard on the back and the hips to be sitting all the time.

I have three cats who see to it that I get up and move around occasionally. They will go outside when I get the paper in the morning, and sometimes, they'll stay outside for a while so I leave the door cracked open so that I can hear them when they are ready to come back in. Sometimes, they decide to come in when I'm in a good spot in my book. There is a moment when I must decide whether to finish the page or get up to let them in. It boils down to which is more important—the welfare of my best friends or seeing what will happen next in my book.

Most of life involves these moments of decisions—do I follow the ruts I've created, or do I move from my comfort zone to help someone else? If we look back at our lives, we sometimes realize that we wouldn't have much without the help of someone else. We tend to help others without even thinking about it! If we see someone trying to get in a door and their hands are full, we'll open the door for them. If we see an old lady trying to shovel the snow from her walk, we'll pitch in and help (and sometimes be rewarded with fresh baked cookies!).

It isn't always just physical activity that is needed, however. Sometimes we just need someone to be a presence. People who have lost something important—like a child, a spouse, a best friend, or even a beloved job or family home—need to feel that they are not going through the experience by themselves. The important relationships with other people or places become a part of us, and when we lose them, we lose a piece of ourselves. It's like losing an arm or a leg. How can we manage without?

These moments are when real strength is needed. Can we be strong enough to sit quietly when someone has a need to tell us about their loss? It's easy to toss out a few sympathetic lines and move on to the next task without seeing the person in pain. It's much harder to (metaphorically) get off the couch to be with someone who needs to talk. It can be even more difficult to be with someone who is having a hard time articulating the problem.

The question then becomes how to best help. Should we use our muscles, brains, or hearts?

Buried in the Dirt

"Listen carefully: Unless a grain of wheat is buried in the ground, dead to the world, it is never any more than a grain of wheat. But, if it is buried, it sprouts and reproduces itself many times over. In the same way, anyone who holds on to life just as it is destroys that life. But if you let it go, reckless in your love, you'll have it forever, real and eternal" (John 12:24–25).

One day, when I was in grade school, Mom and I drove by a house with patches of grass sticking up in a sea of dirt with bikes and tricycles and children's toys scattered around the yard. I think probably a couple of dogs were lying in the sunshine and a cat or two was walking around. I remember Mom saying that it was probably the healthiest house in the neighborhood. She explained that the people in that house had been exposed to all kinds of germs and had been able to develop an immunity to them. She had a good point.

Occasionally, I'll come across a perfect day! The sun shines, and there is just a nip in the air to keep me awake. I'll get everything done that needs to be done, and I'll even have time to do some sitting on my couch. I love those days! They don't come often, but I sure enjoy them when they do come!

It has come to my attention recently that I might not enjoy those perfect days as much if I didn't have to swim through muck and mire to reach them! I read an article about "living water." The Bible tells us that Jesus promises to fill us with living water, but what is special about living water? Living water is water that moves. It flows from a source until it comes out of the mouth.

Living water is filled with life. It runs over the ground picking up the nutrients from the soil, it tumbles over rocks, it contains life and brings that life to others. It's probably green with algae, but if the water is living, it moves too fast for the algae to take over. It probably has a slimy bottom that is disgusting to walk on, but it produces life.

Dirt is the same way. Dirt that is not replenished with nutrients becomes barren. Dirt that has been tended, watered, and fed—dirt that is filled with nutrients—is dirt that produces life. Ask any gardener or farmer which kind of dirt they'd rather see on their hands. Sometimes we need to swim through muck and mire to recharge our own batteries.

Change can be good for us. It stirs us up and makes us feel alive! If I only had those "perfect days," I'd soon become bored. I've recently retired, and I can state with conviction that being free from care is much overrated!

Who Will Judge?

"I saw thrones on which were seated those who had been given authority
to judge. And I saw the souls of those who had been beheaded because
of their testimony for Jesus and because of the word of God. They had
not worshipped the beast or his image and had not received his mark
on their foreheads or their hands. They came to life and reigned with
Christ a thousand years. (The rest of the dead did not come to life
until the thousand years were ended.) This is the first resurrection"
(Revelation 20:4–5 NIV).

Revelation talks about a vision sent to John, the apostle, while he
was in exile on the island of Patmos. It covers a lot of territory. The
last chapters talk about how the world will become darker and darker
and enormously bad stuff will happen. Satan is supposed to appoint a
prophet who will rule the world until God decides to shut them both
down.

Satan and his minions are to be locked in a dark place for a thousand
years while God and his armies straighten things out on earth. After
those thousand years, Satan will be let loose upon the earth for one final
confrontation before God sends his holy fire down to save his people.
Satan will then go into torment for eternity.

The thing is, while God gave this vision to John, and possibly to others,
no one really knows what's going to happen. I believe that John was
describing what he saw, but John was speaking from his experience,
and I don't believe that John had experienced the things that were in
his vision. It's like asking a blind person to describe a mountain lake.

That person can describe how it sounds, smells, and feels, but not what it looks like.

I have a small problem with the idea of people judging people. Too often, we look at the surface of a situation and make decisions based on what we see. There is a saying about icebergs—that we only see 10 percent of the top of the iceberg, and it's the 90 percent underwater that can cause the most damage. People are the same way. The visible part of us is only 10 percent. Only God can see the 90 percent that's going on inside of us!

We have so much inside of us, and many times we don't understand why we do the things we do. How could someone who can't possibly know what's going on in my mind judge the actions that stem from that place?

The only one who can correctly judge anyone is God. He's the only one who can see into the heart of things to determine why we do what we do. I have a feeling that God will open his heart and his mind to those sitting in judgment during this thousand-year period—interestingly called the Millennium! That's the only way for the judgments to be correct.

It will take a brave soul to be a part of this!

Time to Break Out

"Meanwhile, the ministry of God's Word grew by leaps and bounds" (Acts 12: 24).

It's an interesting story behind this scripture. Four generations of Herods tried to squelch Jesus and his followers. The last one killed James, the apostle John's brother, and had Peter arrested. An angel came to get Peter out of jail and, when Herod called for him the next day, Peter was not to be found. Herod ordered the execution of the jailers who had been responsible for Peter, and then Herod decided to leave town.

We can find ourselves in a position like Peter. We're imprisoned by our culture or the expectations of others. Sometimes we are bound by our own expectations! We have standards that we expect to follow, but those expectations can drain us of our energy.

Expectations are supposed to provide a path along which we can walk in confidence. If we follow that path, we're supposed to end up as the good guys! We're supposed to be nice to old ladies and little puppies. We're supposed to take care of God's children. What if, by following the path of expectations, we end up looking for old ladies and puppies to take care of and forget to take care of our own families?

I met a fellow who was a lifeguard at a swimming pool during the summer. He told me that one of the hardest things when trying to save someone is when that someone tries to help. He said that it is often better if the person being saved is unconscious during the process.

Following that path of expectations is like trying to help while we're being saved. Those early Christians didn't know what to expect. Most of them were Gentiles, and they didn't know the many rules the Jews had followed for centuries.

Herod and his Jewish advisers knew the path of expectations so well that they could follow it in their sleep! When the Gentile followers of Jesus came, dancing along a different path, the "old guard" didn't know what to do. They flipped and flopped around trying to gain control of these new Christians and were thwarted at every turn.

What would happen if we left that path of expectations and took God at his word? Psalm 23 says that God will lead us in paths of righteousness. Psalm 32 says that God will instruct us in the ways we should go. Those Gentile followers of Jesus did just that. They expected God to take care of the world, and that's when God's Word grew unbelievably. God was able to save his children without knocking them out first!

It isn't easy finding our own paths. We fall and become discouraged, but, if we get up again and keep walking along our path, holding fast to God's hand and listening to his words, we can find treasures beyond counting. It's better than getting knocked out so that God can save us!

Married Again

"When Christ died, he took that entire rule-dominated way of life down with him and left it in the tomb, leaving you free to 'marry' a resurrection life and bear 'offspring' of faith for God" (Romans 7:4).

I got married in 1975 because that's what women did. Somehow, I had it in my mind that women got married, had babies, and stayed with the family they created for the rest of their lives (and the women in my family lived long lives!) Looking back, I don't think I necessarily loved the fellow I married. I loved the story I had written about our lives more than I loved the people involved in the story.

Unfortunately, this story didn't have the ending that I had anticipated. My husband and I became more like roommates than family. We stopped talking with each other and started talking to each other—without listening to what the other was saying.

As the years went by, I came to realize that we didn't have anything in common—except our address. I started to realize that we were wasting our lives by staying together just because married couples were supposed to stay together. It came to me that we needed to be set free from each other so that we could meet people who could help us become the people we were created to be—to help us grow! So, we got divorced.

There are some people who believe in rules—not as guides to behavior, but as ways to live. Just as I thought it was a rule that women were supposed to get married and have children, some people take the rules of the Old Testament as a way of life. This isn't wrong—if it touches your heart. It can be a problem if you live by these rules only because they're rules, not looking at the reasons for the rules.

For example, we follow the rules for worshipping God, not because we have come to know God but because we hope that following the rules will allow us to live with God. Which comes first, the rules or the worship?

In Matthew 5:17, Jesus says that he has come not to abolish the law but to fulfill it. If we try to keep the word of the law, without keeping the heart of the law, why did Jesus have to die and be resurrected?

I think that when Jesus came to earth, walked among us, died, was buried, and came back from the dead, he separated us from our first "spouse"—the law. The law doesn't necessarily bring us closer to God but can divert our attention away from God. Once we realize that we can approach God individually, directly, we can develop a relationship with God, rather than developing a relationship with the law. We are free to "marry" God and to become the people we were created to be! We can find a family that is filled with life!

The Mark of Passion

"As all those who sat on the High Council looked at Stephen, they found they couldn't take their eyes off him—his face was like the face of an angel!" (Acts 6:15).

When my brother was starting out in grade-school sports, Mom was worried because she might have to miss some of Rob's games. A friend of hers told her not to worry about it. "If you miss a game, just ask him how it went!" was the advice. "He'll love telling you, and you'll learn what he thinks is important!"

Have you ever watched a child describe a game that they played or an injustice that they suffered? Their eyes become bigger as they become involved with the story. Their hands start to move, and then their whole body takes over while they demonstrate "exactly" what happened.

It's seldom that we see an adult become enthusiastic about something; but when we see some people who start talking about the plight of abandoned animals, the state of Congress, or a new grandchild, their eyes start to get bigger, their hands start to move, and pretty soon, their whole body becomes engaged. The great orators, actors, artists, musicians, and leaders have the capacity to share the passion of their visions with others, and we can see those visions—at least for a time.

After Pentecost, the followers of Jesus increased by leaps and bounds. The apostles decided to get organized, and a group of people were chosen to take care of the physical needs of the followers so that the apostles could continue caring for the spiritual needs. Stephen was one of the people chosen. He was so filled with passion for his duties that amazing things were done by him.

As is often the case, a small group of people didn't like the popularity of Stephen so they decided to take him to court. They bribed some witnesses to twist Stephen's words into falsehoods that would lead to his death. Stephen's passion led him through his trial and his death. Passion will do that.

Sometimes it seems like we live in a world of extremes. Either we are surrounded by dull gray people who are trying to be reserved to the point of lifelessness, or we are surrounded by people who have no sense of restraint. They splash the world with discordant colors that clash and grate against each other, and they deafen us with words of great passion but no meaning.

There should be a nice middle place where the words we hear and the colors we see enlighten our lives. They should bring us out of dullness and up to where we can see the sun, but not bring us up so high that we lose touch with the earth.

It has been said that people don't care how much you know until they know how much you care! The only way to change the world is to show people what you care about. Once you start talking about your passions—beekeeping, finances, or baseball—people will start listening. When people start listening, things start happening. Let your light shine, but be careful that your colors don't clash!

Momentum Counts for a Lot

"Their suspicions didn't slow Saul down for even a minute. His momentum was up now, and he plowed straight into the opposition, disarming the Damascus Jews, and trying to show them that this Jesus was the Messiah" (Acts 9:22).

This passage takes place after Saul's conversion on the road to Damascus. Saul was such a radical traditionalist that he was sending new Christians to jail because they didn't agree with his theology. He goes to Damascus to round up a bunch of these "rebels" and meets Christ on the road. After that experience, Saul begins preaching to the same people he had originally been trying to crush. Why would any of them listen to this man?

It's interesting that all the great movements in history—the rise of Britain after William the Conqueror, the consolidation of China, both the rise of Hitler and his downfall, the Revolutionary War—have started with one person who spoke a truth reflected by the people.

People can say that countries are run by their governments, but in reality, the governments (even dictatorships) are reflections of the people. When the people who clean our streets or deliver our mail or wash our clothes, the ones who sell us goods and services, the ones who sit in the pews or watch parades—when all these people are ready to hear a truth, it just takes one person speaking that truth to light a fire in the countryside.

Saul was the match for that time and place. He began to speak truth to all who would hear and ended up spreading the word about Jesus Christ beyond the Jewish religion into the world. He became known as Paul.

It takes courage, passion, and faith to declare your belief, and you'd better really believe what you're saying. If you're just paying lip service to a platitude, you won't be able to develop the momentum to carry you out of your house.

I believe that God gives us a word to speak. If we are brave enough to speak that word, I believe that God will use that word to change lives. Some people have been given a word of encouragement to speak, some have been given a word of prophecy or of direction. If we ignore the words we're given, it's like a bunch of lint is stuck in the dryer vent, and a fire hazard is created. If we speak the words we're given, God can use that to generate momentum in the countryside, and amazing things can happen. It only takes a spark!

Unfortunately, with the wildfires that have ravaged Australia, the Amazon forest, and California, we can see the destructive power of fire out of control. Speak the words God has given you. If you aren't sure that your words come from God, ask him. He will be quick to answer you. Give him control, and watch the world change!

Wide Receivers

"Make sure you get this right: Receiving someone I send is the same as receiving me, just as receiving me is the same as receiving the One who sent me" (John 13:20).

I must admit, I don't know much about football. In fact, I only go to the high school football games because my friend tells me that we need to support the high school team. We sit in the bleachers and watch the opposing teams struggle with each other up and down the field. We watch the cheerleaders stirring up the enthusiasm of the crowd to cheer on their team. We watch the spectators become involved in the game, leaning forward as if to help the players run faster and yelling encouragement. Because we don't always follow the action correctly, we have found one cheer that we can yell with confidence—Go team!

However, when a quarterback throws the football down the field, and it is caught by a player who then runs like mad for the goal post, I jump up, screaming and yelling with the rest of the crowd. There is something magical in those long throws when the ball spirals up in the air and sails gracefully into the receiver's hands.

I looked up "wide receiver" because I wanted to know what they did. Wikipedia says that a wide receiver is an offensive—not a defensive—position in football. It's used when you want to gain ground, not defend it. Those in this position separate themselves from the crowd of players so that they can catch those long passes. That sounds like what John was talking about in this passage.

When God wants to spread his message far and wide, I think that he looks for "wide receivers." Those who stand outside the crowd, who have space to see what's going on and to listen for God's moments. So often we become caught up in daily living, and we don't take the time to really see the world around us in its beauty and majesty.

It isn't a coincidence that many of the great prophets went apart from the crowds. Jesus, himself, sought time alone with God. It doesn't take much to find some time alone. Sometimes it's a matter of taking a deep breath, watching a child sleeping, or walking in the garden in the cool of the day. Sometimes it's driving over long roads by yourself on the way to a job. It could be a song that stirs your heart or a piece of art that speaks to you. It could be a memory of someone no longer near.

In these alone times we can quiet our minds and hearts to hear the voice of God more clearly. We can receive what he has to say to us. Like those wide receivers, we can catch what God sends us, tuck it safely into our hearts, and run wildly for the goal posts.

Great Responsibility

"Every high priest selected to represent men and women before God and offer sacrifices for their sins should be able to deal gently with their failings since he knows what it's like from his own experience. But that also means that he has to offer sacrifices for his own sins as well as the people's. No one elects himself to this honored position. He's called to it by God, as Aaron was" (Hebrews 5:1–4).

When I was teaching, I used to get irritated with people who dismissed teachers as ones who did nothing. Some people had the impression that teachers assigned pages to be read and then walked around the classroom with a ruler, ready to whack some unsuspecting student on the head for not reading properly. Not only did we sit around all day, I was told, but we had three months off in the summer, a week off at Christmas and at Easter, and lots of days off for in-service days.

While there may be some "teachers" who will do this, most of the real teachers I know do not. We may assign pages to be read, and we may be walking around the classroom, but that's to gauge which students are understanding the reading material—not for whacking purposes.

The kids may have three months off for summer, but it usually takes a good month to close out the books when school is over, a good month to gear up for the upcoming year, and the remaining month is spent on taking classes to remain certified. The days off during the school year are days off for kids—not teachers. We're busy listening to new methods of teaching or trying to figure out what the Department of Education wants to promote for the current year. We're busy planning how we can fit this new information into an already full day.

I have found preaching to be much the same as teaching. While there are some preachers who find their sermons online and read them on Sundays, many preachers ponder on scriptures throughout the days prior to presenting the sermon. It is a twenty-four-hour per day, seven days a week calling, just like teaching. The preparation may be different, but the dedication is the same. No one goes into either profession to become rich or famous.

Those who stand in the gap between people and God are just like everyone else. We are brave, we are cowards, we are honest, and sometimes we lie. Sometimes we're energetic, and sometimes we're lazy. Sometimes we know what we're doing, but mostly we haven't a clue. About the only thing that we have in common is a developing relationship with God. Does that sound familiar? Have you also been there? If so, it's possible that you are also doing some preaching without realizing it. We do the best that we can and depend upon God to make up what we're lacking. It seems to work!

The Prodigal Dad

"The Father loves the Son extravagantly. He turned everything over to him so he could give it away—a lavish distribution of gifts" (John 3:34).

The definition of the word *prodigal*, according to my internet, is: "spending money or resources freely and recklessly; wastefully extravagant," "having or giving something on a lavish scale." We often hear the story of the prodigal son, where the son demands his inheritance so that he can go see the world. He packs up his goods and heads out—to find himself later with nothing because he has spent it all on passing fancies.

We hear how we are like this son who takes his inheritance for granted, squandering it on things that don't last. Many of us are like this son. Some are like the older son who stayed home, dutifully fulfilling responsibilities and trudging through life as though joy were sinful, and there were no reasons to celebrate. Both sons could be described as "prodigal," wasting opportunities because they were "reckless" with their time. Neither of them wanting to really know the father.

I heard a sermon based on the prodigal son in Luke 15 where the minister said that it was actually the father who was prodigal. The father gave his younger son money to which he was not yet entitled and welcomed him later when the son came crawling back. The father also gave his older son whatever he asked for, saying, "All that is mine is yours."

The story of the prodigal son is often used to describe the relationship between God—the Father—and his children. We come to him, either asking or not asking. We sometimes treat him as a butler or an ATM machine, expecting him to give us whatever we ask. Sometimes we don't ask for anything. We just go about his business with an air of martyrdom, remarking about our sainthood. We go to God reminding him of all the good that we've done and showing the scars we received in "his service." In neither case do we take time to get to know him. We're often so busy living our lives that we don't think about the One who gave us life.

God has command of everything! His resources and power are infinite, and he gave all this to his Son, Jesus. The very Son who went to the cross to die for us so that we might be able to come to God as we are, knowing that we are loved beyond death!

We are surrounded by so much love from our God that it is impossible to comprehend. We're not always given to understand the reason why we must swim through hard times, why we end up facing heartache, disaster, and trauma. If we call out, however, we discover that we are not going through these times alone. God and his Son are with us all the way and will celebrate with us on the other side, knowing that we will come out victorious!

Why Are We Here?

"Don't be flip with the sacred. Banter and silliness give no honor to God. Don't reduce holy mysteries to slogans. In trying to be relevant, you're only being cute and inviting sacrilege" (Matthew 7:6).

I don't believe that this piece of scripture is saying that we can't have fun with God. I think God enjoys a good joke. I believe that God loves spending time with us. He likes camping and staying at elegant hotels. He loves football, basketball, rugby, and lacrosse. He also likes listening to music: rap, jazz, classical, country, and rock. He can dance like nobody's business. He loves art —even those pieces that don't seem to make sense!

I've had some great discussions with God. Sometimes I'll share a joke with him, and he laughs just as hard as I do. Sometimes I just chat with him, telling him about my day and thanking him for getting me to the gas station before I ran out of gas or getting me home before the storm hit. Sometimes I ask him questions like, "Why are people like this, God? Why are some people so focused on hurting others?"

People can be so strange, can't they? There is so much anger and fear in this world. It sometimes seems like people are working so hard to make everyone just like them that they don't see the wonder in our differences.

Not everyone can be a leader. You can't lead unless someone follows you. We can't all be organized, or there wouldn't be anything for organized people to put in order. If everyone put their socks in the sock drawer, those tidy souls who feel compelled to clean up after us would soon get bored. We need people who can cook and people who can eat. We need people who like beer, people who like wine, and people who are happy with a good bottle of water.

We need nice, kind people in this world, but we also need to have some people who aren't so nice. Sometimes mean people can get a point across faster than a nice person. Nice people do a lot of talking, but some of us are a little hardheaded, and we won't change our ways unless someone comes along and forces us to stop and think.

We need people who are honest with themselves. So many of us tend to fudge the truth when it comes to ourselves. I read once that when people look in the mirror, they tend to stand in ways that make them look thinner. How often do you stand square in front of the mirror? We tilt our heads in certain ways to hide that double chin or the turkey neck.

This is a big world, and it needs all of us in it. The world would be a much sadder place to live in if you weren't there. Know that God loves you so much! He created you for a reason. He knew you would be necessary.

Grrr

"Go ahead and be angry. You do well to be angry, but don't use your anger as fuel for revenge. And don't stay angry. Don't go to bed angry. Don't give the Devil that kind of foothold in your life" (Ephesians 4:26–27).

I love this scripture. So often we get the impression that we are supposed to be nice all the time, put on a smile for the public and ignore the anger that can bubble up inside of us. If we don't get angry at injustice or cruelty, they will just continue—more than that, they will grow.

Anger is a cleansing emotion. Unlike discontent or irritation, anger gets right to the point. Discontent and irritation are fuzzier emotions. We don't always know the reasons why we feel them. It's like having itchy skin in that you keep scratching the itch, but the itch doesn't go away until it's good and ready.

Anger can sweep the field clear. Anger can have a focus and can get things done. Granted, we need to be careful with our anger so that it doesn't goad us into dangerous behaviors. This is also addressed in this scripture. We need to control our anger so that it becomes righteous, not uncontrollable like wildfire.

In this part of the country, we see controlled burns when our fields need to be cleared off. These controlled burns can transform ground cover into fertilizer so that when the new crops are planted, they have room to grow. There is less competition for the minerals in the soil so they can get a good start.

These burns are more than just lighting a fire on a plot of ground that needs to be cleared. You only want to burn off what needs to be burned. If you just start a fire and walk off, nothing is accomplished but destruction. Nothing is gained. The only way to get the good from the fire is to pay attention to it, being prepared to stop it when it starts to get out of hand. If you let it go too long, it will burn the good along with the bad.

Anger, used correctly, can be like those controlled burns. It can clear off the playing field, getting rid of the sticky power plays or the insidious snarky remarks that don't promote anything but only serve to irritate and encourage discontent. We need to say what needs to be said and then we need to walk away for a time. We need to let the dust settle and to see what changes may have occurred. We may have to walk back into the situation with more anger, but we shouldn't let the anger consume us. Don't go to bed angry. You may have to stay up late processing the anger, but don't take it to bed with you. It's hard to sleep when you're visioning all the rotten things you'd like to do to teach "them" a lesson!

A Promise of Rest

"The promise of 'arrival' and 'rest' is still there for God's people. God himself is at rest. At the end of the journey we'll surely rest with God" (Hebrews 4:9–10).

(Author's note: This article was written in early November 2020, during the early days of the pandemic. In an effort to avoid other people—and thereby avoid the disease—most everything was either closed, canceled, or adapted so that it was done online. With fewer things to do physically, our minds seemed to speed up and work overtime. Either we were worried about our jobs and finding ways to make ends meet or we were worried about our families and how they were coping with the change in the world. This time seemed to reaffirm the idea that mental effort can be just as tiring as physical effort—if not more so!)

I don't know about you, but the idea of rest feels pretty good! I don't know why it is that, with the coming of the COVID virus, when we're supposed to stay away from people, and everything is closing down, I'm more tired now than I have been in the past when I had several meetings every day with deadlines looming. With fewer meetings and more time off, I thought I would be better rested by now.

In the beginning, it was hard to turn my mind off from plotting and planning the next day's business. I'd check my calendar to see what I had for the next day, and then I'd start calculating when I needed to get up so that I could get everything done. When would be a good time to go to the grocery store so that I could run to the bank and still have time to write articles, clean the basement, wash the kitchen floor, and do laundry?

I noticed, however, that my carefully planned schedules seem to be blown apart. I would plan to work in the yard on Saturday. I planned to mow the yard, trim the shrubs, and water the grass, only to have it rain all day. I would plan to run all my errands only to have phone calls from fellow workers or my boss or family or friends and never make it to my car.

Lately, however, I've decided to stop planning my day. I still have appointments that I try to keep, but I no longer schedule every minute of the day. Saturdays are no longer the days when I clean the house and work in the yard. I've learned how to mow a little bit every day. I can do laundry during the week when I have a whole load.

I remember when my family would take vacations. Dad liked to see the country, so every year we'd go someplace. Every other year, we'd take longer trips, to the East Coast or the West Coast, to Canada or to the Gulf of Mexico. Every night along the way, we'd stop at a motel to have supper and to just sit for a while before going to bed. Every day was an adventure, but every night we could lay the day down and rest up.

While this scripture seems to be talking about resting with God at the end of our lives, I don't think we need to die before we can rest. There used to be a saying, "There's no rest for the wicked, and the righteous don't need it." I don't think that's correct. I think that both the wicked and the righteous need to rest occasionally—when they can lay their troubles down for a minute or two and just be.

A Good City

[God says] "Old men and old women will come back to Jerusalem, sit on benches on the streets and spin tales, move around safely with their canes—a good city to grow old in. And boys and girls will fill the public parks, laughing and playing—a good city to grow up in. ... Do the problems of returning and rebuilding by just a few survivors seem too much? But is anything too much for me? Not if I have my say" (Zechariah 8:4–6).

(Author's note: This article was written in November 2020. While our country hadn't been invaded by an army from another country, we had been transported into a new world. In a way, we had just as many different approaches to life as the Judeans when those who had been in exile were sent home. There were many different announcements from people who had the credentials to sound credible. Some physicians were not seeing the high death rates from COVID as were reported in New York or Florida and were promoting a less panicked response to the pandemic. Some physicians were seeing people dying on the streets and promoted a different approach. It seemed for a while that we received different directives every day, and everyone had to choose which directives they would follow.)

The Babylonians decided that they wanted the land of Judah, so they brought their armies in and took over the country. They rounded up all the government people who knew what was going on behind the scenes. The teachers and doctors, the inventors and visionaries, the mayors of the towns, the city councils and the school boards were all shipped off to Babylon. Those who were left behind had to "reinvent the wheel" and keep going.

At the end of seventy years, there was an upset in Babylon, and the conquerors were conquered. Cyrus came into power and decided that the Jews needed to go home. After seventy years, the children who had left Jerusalem were now old men and women. The government people who knew the alliances that needed to be maintained for the good of Judah now knew other people—people who dealt with Babylon. Teachers and doctors had kept on learning and helping others because that's what teachers and doctors do; but they were used to new schools and treatments. Very few people remembered what it was like in Judah.

Even worse, those who were left behind had developed a life that suited them. There were new mayors, city councils, and school boards dealing with the new life in Judah. New teachers and doctors were helping the new kids who didn't remember what it had been like before.

We haven't had the COVID virus for seventy years yet, but there are some similarities between our world and the world of the Jews when Cyrus sent everyone home. There are a lot of coaches who are trying to figure out athletic seasons when there's no schedule that can be followed because we don't know when a team will have to cancel due to quarantines. Teachers and doctors and lawyers are trying to figure out new systems with changing rules. Production has changed because of shutdowns, so some items that we rely on are no longer available. Instead of getting what we order, we now get what we are sent.

During all this confusion, one thing remains the same. God is still in charge. Oh, there is another thing that hasn't changed. When Mel Gibson's movie *The Passion of the Christ* came out, my dad went to see it. I asked him what he thought about it. He said, "I've read the book. We win in the end." That hasn't changed either.

Family Stars

[God says] "I will pour on the house of David and on the inhabitants of Jerusalem the Spirit of grace and supplication; then they will look on Me whom they pierced. Yes, they will mourn for Him as one mourns for his only son and grieve for him as one grieves for a firstborn" (Zechariah 12:10 NKJV).

Every family has at least one superstar. My great-grandmother's brother ended up in Alaska where he found a way to bring reindeer to North America from Siberia. He later organized a herd of reindeer and drove it up the Alaskan coast to a ship that had been stranded in ice, and he saved the expedition.

The problem with superstars is that we tend to become fixated on their one heroic deed and don't see the complicated behaviors and thought patterns that don't fall in line with our perception of "the hero." The Jews became fixated on David. They admired his rise from shepherd to king but tended to gloss over the hardships he faced on that journey to fame. They recognized his love of God but overlooked his love of women.

All that we have left of my long-ago uncle is a couple of newspaper clippings telling how he was a superintendent of schools in northern Alaska and how he saved that ship. He ended up writing a couple of books, but they are no longer in print, so there is, essentially, nothing left of him except as an interesting footnote in history.

King David's family, however, included someone who would shine far brighter and whose influence would extend far wider than David.

There are two sets of prophecies in the Old Testament dealing with Jesus. One set declares the majesty of Christ. He will come in glory and take over the world. He will bring peace and prosperity to the land, and all will dwell in harmony. These prophecies have been popular ever since they were first uttered.

The other set declares the sorrow of Christ—how he would be mistreated, beaten up, slaughtered as a sacrificial lamb. These prophecies weren't as popular. When they were fulfilled, many people didn't pay any attention.

After his resurrection and ascension into heaven, the star of Jesus continued to burn brighter and steadier. Rather than a comet that shoots through the sky and falls to the earth when it has burned out, the star of Jesus grew until he now influences the whole earth.

Many Jews regret how Jesus was treated the first time he came to earth. Many have converted to Christianity and now follow him. As has been said before, hindsight is usually 20/20. Looking back, we can see where we should have turned right instead of left or where we should have turned around and gone back.

My mom used to say that everyone shines at some point in their lives. The earlier in your life that you shine, the earlier that you're likely to burn out. The best time to shine is at the end of the day.

Everything Will Be OK

"That night the Master appeared to Paul: "It's going to be all right. Everything is going to turn out for the best" (Acts 23:11).

(Author's note: This was written in November 2020. The confusion surrounding the pandemic continued, and the angry voices got louder. Violence erupted like small fires around the country. It wasn't like a wildfire because the incidents weren't particularly related, and they occurred in many different places under many different circumstances for many different reasons. It almost felt like they were designed to be irritating, and they accomplished that goal. The world may be settling down, but we're still faced with confusion as to what it is settling down to become.)

The older I get, the more I can relate to Paul. I really didn't like him much when I first started reading scripture. It seemed like he didn't have much use for women, and he seemed to be totally convinced that he was smarter than God. He followed all the rules, studied under the smartest teachers (probably getting straight As), and decided to show everyone the error of their ways. However, I read a piece on Paul one time that pointed out that his letters showed a growing humility. Then there is his famous passage in Romans 7:15: "For what I try to do, I end up not doing and I end up doing what I hate instead."

I've been there a lot of times. It seems like the more I try to do the right thing, the "wronger" I find myself. There is a saying to the effect that good intentions will not always lead us to heaven. If good intentions won't get me where I'm trying to go, what will?

This scripture comes after Paul has been arrested in Jerusalem. He had been in the temple helping some people with purification rites and was attacked. The Roman guards came to his rescue, taking him out of the temple. This was the incident that sent Paul to Rome. Paul was beaten severely by the Jews and threatened with torture by the Romans. He was pretty much at the end of his rope when Jesus comes to him to let him know that everything is going to be fine.

Sometimes, I wonder if anything will ever be fine again. We have conflicting reports coming out about the COVID virus, we have conflicting reports coming out about the election, we have conflicting reports about violence around the country. One set of "experts" says to go right while another set of "experts" says to go left, and the next thing you know, the "experts" are yelling at each other, and no one seems to know what they are saying. Sometimes I want to join in the yelling matches, but I can't see that adding one more voice to the uproar would help anything.

People handle this situation in various ways. Some people join in the yelling, some people bake cookies, some people go shopping. I tend to sit in my house and watch a movie or read a good book. Sometimes I read my Bible, and when I do, I come across scriptures of peace and strength and hope and encouragement like this one.

It is a comfort to know that God has a plan for this world. It's a relief to know that someone is in control, and I can't think of anyone better to be in control than God! Just hang tight, it's going to be all right. The plan is working.

At Some Point, We Have to Leave the Classroom

"You know your way around the faith. Now do what you've been taught. School's out; quit studying the subject and start living it! And let your living spill over into thanksgiving" (Colossians 2:7).

For some of us, there is no safer place than in a classroom. If you're in a classroom, you know that there are answers to all the questions somewhere—in a book or in a person standing at the head of the classroom. If you're the one standing at the head of the class, you know that somewhere, in a book or on a computer, there is an answer to all the questions likely to be asked of you. The answers may not be proven—they may just be theories or good guesses, but if the questions are asked in a classroom, we can talk about theories without having experience of them.

The problem with classrooms is that, at some point, the answers to the questions must be verified in real life. The theory that one plus one equals two should be proven before we can rely on it—and it is generally reliable (until you come to some situations where it doesn't work—for example one dandelion plus one dandelion equal many more than two dandelions!).

Experience becomes the teacher—and an excellent teacher she is! Once you have walked a mile in the pouring rain, you learn to carry an umbrella (or take the car). We know what our religion says about God, but do we really believe what our religion tells us? The difference between "faith" and "religion" is that faith comes from experience.

We can't tell people how God is always with us unless we have felt his presence in our difficulties as well as in our victories. When we have seen his light at the end of our tunnels and have followed that light out of the darkness, we can state with assurance that God is always with us.

The thing is, we're not likely to be in difficult situations when we're sitting in a classroom. Those situations come when we're out of school and there are no books or computers or people standing at the head of the class. Those situations come when we're living.

We may not be too excited when we're getting the experiences, but those experiences can be lifesavers for others who may be looking at similar situations. The best help for people who have been hurt are those people who have been hurt and have risen above it, when we start to live our faith.

If you have been in a bad relationship and have broken free of it or if you have learned the courage to be yourself, you have so much to offer others. This world desperately needs people who will live their faith boldly. At the end of the day, those people will be deeply appreciated!

Are You Sure?

"If we claim that we experience a shared life with [God] and continue to stumble around in the dark, we're obviously lying through our teeth—we're not living what we claim" (1 John 1:6–7).

I sometimes have problems with leaders of Bible studies. Quite often, their studies are based on books written by someone else who has done a lot of research on a subject and has put that research into print. There are open-ended questions that are designed to make us think, but there are also answers to those questions that suggest each question has one correct answer.

With all the diversity that God has created, how can each question have only one correct answer? If a hummingbird is faced with being eaten by a larger animal, its answer would be different than a tiger who is faced with being eaten. The bird can fly away while the tiger has weapons—like muscles, claws, and teeth. Even if we stick with the same species, there are different responses to danger—some people will run and hide while others will come out with all guns blazing. All these responses are correct responses to the question, "What should you do when someone tries to eat you?"

I was talking with a lady the other day who was in the same situation I have experienced—only at a different time. We were both invited by friends to visit the French Quarter in New Orleans for the purpose of inspecting voodoo dolls. We chose different answers to the question. Her answer was no—because God had told her to avoid dangerous situations. My answer was "OK" —because God promised to never leave me. Both answers were correct.

It's entirely likely that her friend needed to hear that someone would care enough to keep boundaries. Someone needed to show her friend that there are other options and that staying safe is important. In my case, it was important for me to trust that God will go everywhere with me. He will guard me and protect me no matter what. His power is greater than any other power that exists. It was also important to me that my friend did not go by herself. I wanted her to know that I had her back—just like God had mine.

One thing, however, was consistent in these two different responses— we both checked with God first. Sharing our lives with God means including him. We take his hand and expect him to lead us down the path he has laid out for us—even if it leads through the French Quarter. If we claim to share our lives with God, we may stumble around in the dark for a bit, but if we have developed a personal relationship with him, we can trust that our responses will be correct—even if they don't match the answers in the book—and we won't stumble around for long.

Let's Try This Again

"Attention all Israelites! The Word of the Lord! God indicts the whole population: 'No one is faithful. No one loves. No one knows the first thing about God'" (Hosea 4:1).

I have a very good friend who is trying to help me become healthier. She knows that I have a sweet tooth that has been allowed to have its own way for some time now and has grown almost bigger than my mouth. I invited her to come with me to run an errand out of town, and when we stopped off at a fast-food restaurant, she asked me what I wanted to get. When I told her that I wanted an ice cream cone, she gave me this stern look and asked what I'd had for lunch. I hated to tell her that I had eaten several Tootsie Rolls and other candy, so I told her I had had some frosted cookies (thinking that their more complex carbohydrates might make them healthier). She bought me a hamburger. While it didn't taste quite as good as an ice cream cone, I did feel better after I ate the hamburger.

It's nice to have people tell us how great we are, how smart and kind we are, but sometimes we're better off when we're told the truth. I may believe myself to be a great cook, but I have come to realize that if I'm going to feed other people, it's better if I buy the food already prepared.

Our real friends are the ones who carefully tell us the truth about ourselves. They are the ones who gently tell us that even though that polyester pant suit was great in its day, it's time to give it a decent burial. They will agree with us that Aunt Muriel's behavior is becoming decidedly odd, but we probably shouldn't smack her upside the head.

This is what God is doing to the Israelites in our scripture for today. After Solomon died, the country split into the northern kingdom of Israel and the southern kingdom of Judah. The people living in the north became tired of traveling to the other side of the country to conduct their business, so they decided to set up their own country. Unfortunately, in the process, they forgot the God they had in common with Judah.

Hosea was the only prophet from Israel—all the others were from the southern kingdom of Judah. While the people of Israel forgot about God, God didn't forget them. Instead of wiping them from the face of the earth and starting over from scratch, God buys them hamburgers instead of the ice cream cones they ask for. God is the best friend we could ever have (even if we'd rather eat ice cream).

A Holy War

"But then God will march out against the godless nations and fight—a great war!" (Zechariah 14:3).

The Old Testament is filled with stories of how God's children came up against other people—the godless nations that decided to wipe them off the face of the earth. God went to war for his children, and their enemies were never heard of again. It seems that God knows exactly how to wage a war so that when it's over, it's over. When people wage wars, they seem to go on forever.

World War I started in Europe in 1914, and in 1917 the United States became involved. It turns out that a German submarine sank the Lusitania, killing over one hundred American passengers. Information later became known about a telegram suggesting that an alliance was being discussed between Germany and Mexico, and the United States, in self-defense, officially joined the allies in WW I—the "War to End All Wars." There haven't been many years of peace since then.

While there hasn't been a global war since World War II, the globe seems to be continually at war. Even when countries aren't fighting countries, there seem to be wars going on in our cities and atrocities are committed even on our prairies, our mountains, our deserts, and our waterways. Tragedy occurs in our bars, our churches, and our schools. People have been known to shoot others because they're wearing face masks or because they cut in line. So much anger and fear in our world today is ready to lash out in violence.

It's tempting to run out and purchase the latest book promising world peace in seven easy steps; but I think that anything worth doing won't be done easily—no matter how many steps it takes. I had a social studies teacher in middle school who had been in Germany and had heard Adolf Hitler speak. I remember him talking about it and how scared he became because Mr. Garrison found himself agreeing with what Hitler was saying even though he didn't speak German. It's so easy to become caught up in a crowd mentality, carried along with the tide into deeper, darker waters.

The good news is that thanks to Jesus Christ, we are God's children now. The world hasn't changed that much over the years, and we are still coming across "godless nations" wanting to wipe us from the face of the earth. A great temptation is to hoist our flags, beat our breasts, and rush forth into battle. It takes great courage and discipline to stand still and wait for God. If we just want to flex our muscles, we can go around punching out others but, if we want our efforts to make a lasting difference, it's better if we remember the one who wins his battles is God—not us. When the time is right, God will march forth to fight a great battle—and that battle will be won and done.

What Happened?

"Then those who grew up 'in the faith' but had no faith will find themselves out in the cold, outsiders to grace and wondering what happened" (Matthew 8:12).

Rituals and routines are wonderful for many reasons. They can help us to multitask by allowing our muscle memory to keep brushing our teeth at the same time our brains are trying to remember what needs to be done next. Some routines can help us remember the important people in our lives. I don't make macaroni and cheese the same way Mom did, but every time I make it, I remember her.

Church attendance can be a routine that helps us put things in perspective as well as helping us remember; but it can become a problem if we attend because our moms told us it was a good place to meet a spouse. If we're going because we like their social activities, or we want to be part of the in-crowd, and this is where they go, we're missing the point. Choosing a church for an artificial reason is like living on a diet of Tootsie Rolls. Everything is great for a while but then your face breaks out with acne, your clothes don't fit, and you start to develop health issues.

There is nothing wrong with "church hopping." Life is such a complex, confusing, mysterious process. We never know where it will take us. We start out with a nice, comfortable family and, somewhere along the way, we discover that there are monsters in the world, and they wear masks so that we can't always see who they are until they have us in their clutches. Unless we find someplace where we can take our questions and find peace, we're left hanging at the end of long ropes over deep canyons. The sad thing is that we won't have any clue as to how we got there.

After my divorce, I needed to find a church where I could wrestle with my beliefs to discover what I really thought about God and the universe. I went to the phone book and, checking out the listings for churches, I started with the As and worked my way through. In my case, I discovered that the church I grew up in was a good fit for me. It so happened that the church was going through a time of discovery very much like I was, and we "discovered" together.

It may be that your home is in a church other than where you grew up. The thing is, God has provided a place of worship designed for each of us. You may need a more structured church, or you may need a more eclectic church. Know that God has prepared a place for you and, if you pay attention, he will lead you where you need to go. There is nothing like the feeling that you have found your home. You're no longer outside in the cold looking in.

What Have We Done?

"Do not rejoice, O Israel, with joy like other peoples, for you have played the harlot against your God. You have made love for hire on every threshing floor" (Hosea 9:1 NKJV).

My first year in college, I lived in a dorm. It was in the early seventies, I had just graduated from high school, and I wasn't quite used yet to being considered a "woman." Somehow "women" were more sophisticated and worldly than I was. They thought deep thoughts and would troop to Aggieville every evening to drink beer and flirt with the guys.

At that time, there was a tradition of stealing pitchers from the bars. A pitcher of beer would be ordered for a table and, after it had been drunk and just before heading out and back home, someone would find a hiding place to put the empty pitcher and then laugh themselves silly all the way home. Somehow, I decided that this was a rite of passage that I needed to perform so that I could finally "grow up"!

I've always carried a big purse, so I decided to empty it out one night before heading out to Aggieville. It was an awful evening. I don't much like beer, so I had to depend on my friends to help finish off the pitcher, and then I had to find a way to unobtrusively slip this big pitcher into my purse. But the worst part was the feeling that the people working at the bar seemed to be so disappointed in me.

I got home without any fuss, and then the guilt set in. I knew better than to steal! Someone had paid good money for the pitcher that I had just walked away with. I ended up mailing the bar some money and never went there again.

I realize that, as a "coming of age" story, it's relatively small, but it was traumatic for me and still makes me cringe to think of it after so many years. The point is, we were created for a reason. If we try to become someone we're not, we're risking something particularly important. If we were created to be sophisticated people of the world, and we try to become naïve, shy people who stay home, the world will lose out on what we can offer it. If we're created to be quiet, shy people but we try to become sophisticated people of the world, our families and friends will lose out, which will also affect the world. We all become losers when we try to change ourselves to fit in where we don't belong.

The good thing is that God sticks with us like glue no matter what. My mom would say, "If I didn't love you, I wouldn't care." To which I would reply, "Could you love me a little less?" Of course, she couldn't— she loved me totally. God is the same way. If he didn't love us, he wouldn't care—and he loves us totally.

Winter

Winter is the closing of a circle that started in spring. Winter is a time of reflection. We look back on our lives, the choices we made—and why we made those choices. We don't have the drive to action that we had in the past and are happy to just sit and maybe take a nap.

Our bodies start to have minds of their own, and we often are surprised by what they do. We tell our feet to take us to the kitchen to start fixing lunch, and we find ourselves in the bedroom changing sheets.

Winter is a time when we look at our to-do lists and decide to start working on them—after we take a "short" nap. We remember the friends we made along the way, grieving over those who are no longer with us in body and quietly appreciating those who have hung in there.

Winter may be a time of downsizing our houses. Oftentimes, we live by ourselves and don't need five bedrooms any longer. When the kids come for a visit, they stay in a motel with a swimming pool. We look over all that we have accumulated over our lives, deciding which things to keep and which things need to be sent to someone else.

All too soon, we find ourselves fading out. The memories come and go, and we don't always remember names and faces. The love we have known, however, will never leave us, and as winter ends, that love will walk with us into the future.

Wondrous Surprises

"May Jesus, Himself, and God our Father, who reached out in love and surprised you with gifts of unending help and confidence, put a fresh heart in you, invigorate your work, enliven your speech" (2 Thessalonians 2:16–17).

Have you ever been in the middle of a big mess, feeling like you're drowning, and knowing that there is nowhere to turn? A small voice inside your head says, "You got yourself into this mess, you can get yourself out!" but somehow it seems like the only way out is to go through it!

Some cartoons show a hero crossing a lake, avoiding sharks, snapping jaws, punching bags, and a ring of fire before he must rescue the beautiful young maiden! Or there's the bit about the lady tied to the railroad tracks with a speeding train coming! Sometimes we feel like the lady—tied up and helpless, screaming our lungs out for someone to help! Sometimes we feel like the hero trying to rescue the lady, only someone has tied weights to our feet, and we feel like we're running through jelly! Keeping house can feel like this sometimes. It seems like there is always laundry to do or dishes to wash or bills to pay or people to feed. Going to work is the same—you must be nice to the same yucky people! We feel like we're walking five miles through the snow, uphill both ways!

How many times have we paused for a minute in our frantic running around, or in our panicked cries for help, to take a deep breath? How many times, after that breath, have we discovered hidden depths of strength? How many times do we see a mysterious path through our wilderness that could lead to safety? How many times do we realize that this help comes from God?

I was talking with a friend of mine the other day, and she said something interesting. She said that we have always heard that God doesn't give us more than we can handle, but that God always gives us more than we can handle by ourselves! "How else can we learn and grow? How else can we help others through the same difficult situations?"

I think she has a good point! I go walking my merry way along life's path and suddenly find myself teetering on the brink of a canyon, looking down into the gaping jaws of hell and wondering how I am going to get over to the other side? God reaches out in love and surprises me with gifts of unending help and confidence (to paraphrase this scripture)!

Wherever you are in life's journey, may God "put a fresh heart in you, invigorate your work, [and] enliven your speech!" May you hear His voice in your ear, telling you to ignore the depressing voices and to listen to Him!

What Does God Tell You?

"Whether it's right in God's eyes to listen to you rather than to God, you decide. As for us, there's no question—we can't keep quiet about what we've seen and heard" (Acts 4:20).

We have become so security conscious in the world. Before the days of high technology, it was much easier to know the person trying to access our information! People would cut off hands to use the handprints or rip out eyeballs for retinal scans to enter top secret areas.

If we could find a way to link our information to our belief system, however, I think it could become unhackable! Our beliefs are extremely personal. No two people share the exact same beliefs. Some people's beliefs are black and white—this is right, and this is wrong. Some people have more gray areas—this is right, and this is wrong (with some exceptions—there are gradations of right and wrong. It's more of a continuum rather than two absolutes.)

There are articles on the internet about which fast-food restaurant has the best hamburgers or which state has the worst conditions for retirees. The problem is that everyone has different taste buds. Not everyone likes wine and I hate to say it in this part of Kansas, but not everyone likes beer! We can't state categorically that this is best and that is worst. We must make those decisions for ourselves and allow others to make those decisions for themselves.

Another decision that we must make for ourselves is whether God is speaking to us and just what he is telling us to do. If we have ever asked God into our hearts, he comes to stay. He doesn't go shopping around for cheaper rent or a better view! He doesn't care if you have a private swimming pool in your heart or even if you have running water! He can provide his own water of life!

From his place in our hearts, God speaks to each of us. He tells this one to design buildings, and he tells that one to build them. He tells one person to speak to the nations, and he tells that one to make a tuna casserole for a friend in need. If we pay attention to what is in our hearts, and follow that direction, everything will be done in good order and at the proper time.

The thing is, no one can tell you what God wants you, specifically, to do—except you! You are the only one who can listen to your heart to hear what God is saying.

I heard Joseph Prince talking about this once. He said that Bob had come to him saying that God had said that Bob would work for Joseph Prince. Pastor Prince told Bob that it was strange because God hadn't told him about this plan. We can listen to what God is telling us, but that doesn't mean that God is revealing that same plan to someone else! All we can do is the best we can with what we have and trust that God will take care of the rest!

Weddings and Marriages

"Give honor to marriage and remain faithful to one another in marriage" (Hebrews 13:4 New Living Translation).

The famous line in most wedding ceremonies about "Whatsoever God hath joined together, let no man put asunder" comes from Mark 10:9. It comes from an interesting discussion on divorce. Often, when a divorce occurs, this scripture is thrown at the divorcing couple with the force of a stone.

People have a wedding in hope and joy. Nobody has a wedding with the thought that they will ever get divorced unless it's a marriage to save one person from getting killed or deported and even then, there is hope in the ceremony. We don't make those commitments lightly. We believe that, after the wedding, a marriage will emerge.

I have a theory that any couple that God joins together in marriage cannot be separated except by death. There are some married couples who seem to have the knack of staying together through all kinds of difficulties—or possibly these couples are among those that "God hath joined together."

Here's the thing, however, weddings don't guarantee marriages. People have weddings for all kinds of reasons—financial, dynastic, raging hormones, whatever—as well as love.

Some people seem to want the ceremony and the party afterward. They spend months looking for the perfect dress, the perfect location, and the perfect honeymoon spot. A couple of years later when they are facing bankruptcy, their jobs have been moved, and they are now a bicoastal couple, they decide to get divorced. A couple of years after that, they are once again looking for the perfect dress, the perfect location, and the perfect honeymoon spot for another wedding.

Conversely, there are many couples who held their wedding at the courthouse or didn't have a wedding at all but have held on, supporting each other and helping each other through bankruptcies, evictions, miscarriages, ten children, and all the difficulties life can throw at them. They come through and celebrate their fiftieth or seventy-fifth anniversaries with all their families surrounding them.

To me, this is a marriage. It is more than just a wedding. Loyalty is there. The couple may not even particularly like each other, but if someone else says something against one, the other is right there in solidarity. A bond between them cannot be broken.

Weddings can be plotted and planned. Marriages can't. No special recipe for a successful marriage can be detected by humans. Marriages are made by God, and weddings are made by humans.

Weddings are kind of like whipped cream with cherries and nuts and sprinkles. Marriages are more like macaroni and cheese. The whipped cream, cherries, nuts, and sprinkles are pretty and tasty, but they don't last long and too much of them can make a person sick. The macaroni and cheese, however, can glue you back together when you're sick or having a bad day. The macaroni and cheese will stick to your ribs and remind you that you aren't alone.

The Hound of Heaven

"I'm turning you over to God, our marvelous God whose gracious Word can make you into what he wants you to be and give you everything you could possibly need in this community of holy friends" (Acts 20:32).

I heard a song the other day where this fellow was saying that being free in Christ wasn't having the freedom to do what you wanted to do when you wanted to do it. One of the things that always surprises me is how we limit God.

Many people have this attitude that they need to protect God from the crude, rude, and otherwise impossible world that we live in here on earth. I want to ask them if they are talking about the same God who created the universe and everything in it—living and nonliving! Isn't this the same God who opened the earth and swallowed some of the Israelites in the desert? It seems to me that God can pretty much take care of himself and anyone else who calls on his name.

It may be that some people place a great importance on free choice. They give the impression that God needs an engraved invitation from us to move in our lives. I can see that He might want an invitation at the beginning but, once you've invited him into your life, he's there!

Francis Thompson wrote a poem called "Hound of Heaven," which was first published in 1893. It is a really depressing poem. The poet feels that, if he invites God into his life, he will have nothing else. He will walk around in sackcloth and ashes and deep depression. Trying to avoid that fate, the poet talks about how he tries to run away from God.

He goes into deep pits and onto high mountains. He wallows in filth and degradation, but God always finds him. In the end, the poet finally turns around and realizes that God provides him with everything he ever wanted.

Isaiah 49:16 talks about how God has our names tattooed on the palms of his hand. I don't think that he would be quick to remove them. Once we are his, we are his! That being said, we don't have to walk the path of his choosing. We can go our merry way and not pay any attention to him; however, that doesn't mean that he doesn't pay attention to us!

I believe that God has a plan for all of us! I believe that God knows the end from the beginning. I don't believe that there are any surprises for God. I believe that, if you let Him, God will change you so that, eventually, you do have the freedom to do whatever you want, whenever you want to do it because your desire is to follow God's path. You will be free to help others along their way. You will be free to love others as if they were lovable, and the best part is, if you meet up with impossible people, you will be free to give them to God, and he will take care of them as only he can!

What to Do with Disasters

"Get out [of Babylon], my people, as fast as you can, so you don't get mixed up in her sins, so you don't get caught in her doom" (Revelation 18:4).

It is said that the last remaining apostle, John, wrote Revelation while he was in exile on the island of Patmos. People had been trying to get him to shut up about Jesus, but he just kept talking and talking and talking, so they sent him far away in hopes that he wouldn't be heard!

John calls his book a revelation from Jesus Christ to prepare God's children for what will be coming down the pike. This scripture comes from the part of his book that talks about the fall of Babylon. God is telling his children to run away from Babylon—to get out of the area of coming disaster.

The interesting thing about this is that God isn't asking for any help in destroying Babylon. He seems to feel that he can take care of that by himself. What he wants us to do is to get out of his way!

I think that we can probably use this advice today without waiting for the end of the world. If you find yourself in a flood or earthquake or volcanic eruption, the first thing you need to do is get out of the area. It would be nice if you could help others get out as well, but the important thing is to leave the area of destruction.

If a fire starts heading in your direction, you need to get out of its way! You have options if you're a firefighter, but if you aren't trained in evacuation or firefighting procedures, the best thing you can do is to get out. The first thing responders do when they go to a crisis is to get the people and animals out. If we try to stay and help, we're sure to throw a wrench into the whole process.

People who are trained in crisis management have a system figured out that works well for them, and if someone changes or adds to that system, the whole thing can fall apart, and disaster can follow. I have never heard any first responder anywhere who says, "Hey, can you lend a hand here?" Usually you hear them saying, "Please move along in that direction to safety!"

Why do we think that God would need our help if the first responders don't? He's very good at destroying what needs to be destroyed. If we start helping him with the destruction, we're likely to knock out someone or something that is vital to the recovery process.

It isn't just physical disasters that we need to walk away from. We've all known people who are walking disasters waiting to happen! I think the same thing applies here. God doesn't need our help to destroy, but I think that he would be glad for us to help build up!

I have been a walking disaster at different times in my life, and I can speak from experience! If you have nothing in you to help a walking disaster, it's better to walk quietly away. Don't create a fuss and draw attention to the hurting person! Just walk away. If you have a kind word or a prayer for peace, it is gratefully appreciated, but please don't linger!

The thing about us walking disasters is that we will eventually come out of it to make a difference in the world. We might end up being one of your neighbors, or the doctor you need!

Make It Personal

"Friend, you have no idea how good your love makes me feel, doubly so when I see your hospitality to fellow believers. In line with all this I have a favor to ask of you. As Christ's ambassador and now a prisoner for him, I wouldn't hesitate to command this if I thought it necessary, but I'd rather make it a personal request" (Philemon 7–9).

One of the biggest problems I hear about is the growing lack of customer service. People don't have any free time anymore. Too many things need to get done, and too many people need our help!

When we open our places of business, it seems that there are people lined up at the doors waiting to flood inside and carry things off. There's a madhouse of customers all yelling for attention. Or we wait all day for someone to meander into our place of business. They'll wander around the store, picking something up, looking at it, and putting it back down. They may pick something up and come to the register to buy it, but they can't stay because they were just killing time waiting for a meeting that's coming up soon.

We don't talk to each other anymore. People are starving for connection but don't seem to know how to find it. It seems that we are turning more and more to email, text, or social media to create connections with others. Email, texts, and social media are very good at what they were created to be, but they are not built to create connections. They are built to maintain connections.

If you want to know someone, you must experience them. It's best if you can see them face-to-face! To see their expressions when they say something, so that you know if they are serious about what they're saying. Once you have a face-to-face meeting, you have a better feel for their emails and texts. You can visualize their faces when they say something. If you can see a twinkle in their eye when you read what they wrote, you know that this is not a serious comment. Do they write letters? Do they call unexpectedly to see how you're doing? Do they remember important dates?

Granted, not many have seen God face-to-face. That's why it's so easy to be skeptical about one who claims to "know" God. If there is anyone who is personal, it would be God. If we allow it, he comes to each of us in ways that only we can see, hear, or touch. He can open our hearts and minds to the beautiful and wise and troubled around us. There isn't anyone more personal than God. Each of us has our own experience of him that is just ours.

God is the only one who sees us just as we are and loves us. If we can allow ourselves to be real with God, we can learn to be real with others. When we can meet with others authentically, that's when we can build real connections.

Being personal isn't easy, but it's the only way we can reach out and touch someone!

Generic Products

"Don't be lured away from [Jesus] by the latest speculations about him. The grace of Christ is the only good ground for life. Products named after Christ don't seem to do much for those who buy them" (Hebrews 13:9).

There's a growing trend to look for generic brands. The popular name brands are becoming so expensive and, if the generic works as well, why pay the higher price? The issue becomes murky when we talk about fashion or art. In medicines or food, it's merely a matter of chemical reactions. If you don't want to buy a particular brand of pain medication, you could buy a similar brand that has the right ingredients in the correct ratio, and you should be fine.

In the case of fashion or artwork, however, the element of creativity is an expression of an individual. If you try to copy that, you are essentially stealing the part of that person's soul that was involved in that creation!

And then you have products that are just false advertising! These products promise you the sun, moon, and stars but don't deliver any of those. In fact, they can deliver fear and shame.

Some people feel that they have fallen so far away from God that they look for ways to punish themselves. These people look for belief systems that emphasize atonement through actions. Many times, they will have strict laws with accompanying punishments for anyone who doesn't follow the letter of the law.

Some people feel that, to meet with God, they must run away from the world. They carve out places for themselves where they can exist on their own terms. Communes can be examples of these beliefs.

The thing is that Jesus loved us so much that he was willing to die for us—before we were even thought of by the cosmos! We may stray from his side, but he never strays from us! His greatest desire is for us to live in a relationship with him. He asks us to spend time with him—to get to know him!

The best thing about God is that he comes to us where we are. Each of us is in a different place in our lives. Some of us have been nurtured in love, fed, and cared for all our lives. Some of us have known hunger, fear, and uncertainty. God doesn't come to a child in fear the same way he comes to a child who has never known want. He comes to each of us differently, but he comes to each of us.

If we look to find God through other people or through nature without asking God directly how we can find him, we'll find a generic product that may or may not meet our needs. God tells us to ask him for what we need and what we want—then he asks us to wait for an answer. Sometimes that answer comes in seconds and sometimes it comes in decades, but it will come. It may not come in the way we're expecting it, but it will come!

Be sure to ask for him by name! He will cure whatever ails you!

Heaven

"And God will wipe away every tear from their eyes; there shall be no more death, nor sorrow, nor crying. There shall be no more pain, for the former things have passed away" (Revelation 21:4 NKJV).

Everybody has a different idea of what Heaven will be like. Some people look forward to walking on streets made of gold or living in marble palaces. Some would rather walk on lush grass with trees. There are those who long for mountains, beaches, islands in the oceans, or forests.

John 14:2 talks about the many mansions in God's house. Matthew 19:26 talks about how all things are possible with God. If we take God at his word (which is always a good thing), it is entirely likely that each of these environments is possible—at the same time!

Taylor Caldwell published *Dialogues with the Devil* in 1967. It offers an interesting view of both Heaven and Hell. Her book is a series of conversations between Lucifer and the Archangel Michael. Michael asks Lucifer how things are going in Hell, and Lucifer tells him that everything is great! Everyone is forced to do the same thing all the time. The artists copy Michelangelo's artwork, and when they are done, the canvases erase, and they must do it all over again. Builders build the same structures, healers heal the same people of the same diseases, and musicians play the same songs. There is no change or creativity, and everyone is miserable.

Lucifer asks Michael how things are going in Heaven, and Michael talks about people discovering new worlds, creating interesting new art, learning new things. Everything is exciting and growing—"becoming."

There are times when I think this would be the type of Heaven I would enjoy!

No matter which vision of Heaven we have, however, I think that we would all agree that it would be nice to have no more sorrow, no more separation from those we love. To be safe and secure in the place we love would be—well—heavenly!

One of the nicest parts of Caldwell's book is at the end. Lucifer tells Michael that he thinks God is cheating somehow. It seems that some people have been disappearing from Hell. Lucifer thinks that, once a person has joined his kingdom, he should be there forever! Michael smiles.

I like to think that, even in Hell, people can change. I know that sometimes I need a good whack on the head to make me realize the truth. Maybe others do also!

How Can We Be Healed?

"[Jesus] bore our sins in His own body on the tree, that we, having died to sins, might live for righteousness—by whose stripes you were healed" (1 Peter 2:24 NKJV).

Amazingly enough, I think that this is an appropriate scripture for the New Year! When I first saw it, I thought, "Man! I can't use this scripture! It's too *something!*" The more I think about it, however, the more I can see where it could fit in this season!

Christmastime is a good time to reflect on our lives. If we're young and excited about presents under the tree, we think about how great life is to provide us with all this loot! If we're young adults, just out of school, we think about how our lives are finally coming together, and we can see our success on the horizon.

If we have young kids, and we've been working hard to provide a great Christmas for them, we can see how lucky we are to have families because this is what Christmas is all about—families. If we're older and our kids are with their kids, and we're sitting alone in our homes waiting for someone to call and wish us a Merry Christmas, we tend to think back on all those Christmases when we had all the answers. No one told us that the questions of life would change, and now all the answers we had don't fit the questions we're asking!

Being a Christian means to believe that Jesus is the son of God. Part of that is believing that he died on a cross so that we could come to know God on a personal level. But how does that heal us?

We've all known people (and some of us may be those people) who have severe illnesses or disabilities that prevent us from joining wholeheartedly in life's activities. Some have been healed of these diseases, but many have not. If we look at those who are healed, there doesn't seem to be any rhyme or reason for their healing.

Some of those who have been healed have had great faith, but some have not. Some have been healed after undergoing traditional medical treatment or revolutionary treatment that is still being researched. Some have gone to faith healers and been cured. The problem is that not everyone responds to these different treatments.

What about people who have great faith and who pray daily for deliverance from their conditions but are not healed? Everyone comes to their own understanding of biblical healing; but I would like to suggest that there are many kinds of healing.

We can be healed physically, mentally, emotionally, or spiritually. Our families can be healed as well as our country and our world. It's possible that we have given our diseases and infirmities to God, and he has healed us but not in the way we expected. We may still be on crutches or without body parts, but we have been healed of bitterness and hatred. We may still want to punch someone in the nose, but we are now able to see them without making a fist! Perhaps we have been healed financially, or we have started talking to family members we haven't seen in ages. It's possible that you have been healed but just don't know it!

Wherever you are in life, may you know to the depths of your being that you are loved; and that God is working in your life to bring you just what you need for this upcoming new year! May it be a great one for you!

Flattery vs. Compliments

"Those heretical teachers go to great lengths to flatter you, but their motives are rotten. They want to shut you out of the free world of God's grace so that you will always depend on them for approval and direction, making them feel important" (Galatians 4:17).

I read a piece on Facebook about teaching our daughters to distinguish between several attributes of men. One of the things it mentions is teaching them to tell the difference between "a man who flatters her and a man who compliments her" (author unknown).

The idea is that flattery is done to sway your feelings. It doesn't have any basis in truth but is based on presenting a false persona to make you pleasantly aware of someone or something. We talk about clothes that flatter us by making us look taller or thinner or more chic. Flattering hairstyles will camouflage our flat heads or our square jaws. Men are just as susceptible as women.

We do have more confidence when we feel like we're looking good, and I'm not suggesting that we start to wear unflattering outfits or hairstyles. I think we need to decide on a good look for ourselves and to try to stick with that. What bothers me is when we wear outfits that we don't like or don't find comfortable just to please someone else.

There will always be someone who will try to tell us how we should live, how we should dress, what we should eat, who we should condemn. If you honestly agree with them, then you are in good company. The problem is when you don't agree but go along blindly following these people.

Paul had started a church in Galatia. He had set it up according to the experience he had with Jesus Christ, and then he had to leave Galatia and travel on. It came to his attention that a group of people had come to the Galatian church and were changing it to fit their belief. He was furious! The church that he had founded had been based on a personal relationship with Jesus—not a list of religious rites and regulations. A church that had been free was now enslaved.

Flattery can do this to us. When we start paying more attention to what some people are saying than what we know to be true, those people start to control us—a little at a time but, given enough time, we come under their control and are no longer free.

At this beginning of a new year, let's look at ourselves and see that we are courageous, bold, and infinitely loved. Let's see ourselves as God sees us—not as somebody who needs to fit into a box. Jesus died on a cross so that we could come to know him on a personal level. No one in the world knows us like he does. We can believe the compliments he gives us because it isn't flattery!

Personally

"We didn't learn this by reading books or going to school; we learned it from God, who taught us person to person through Jesus, and we're passing it on to you in the same firsthand, personal way" (1 Corinthians 2:13).

I don't think this verse is telling us to stop reading the Bible. I think it's telling us to ask God what he means! The Bible has been translated in so many different languages, and each language has its own meanings for different words. And it isn't just the words that have to be translated—it's the thought behind the words.

There's a famous grouping of words, "A woman without her man is nothing," that can say two different things, depending on the punctuation. "A woman, without her man, is nothing" or "A woman: without her, man is nothing." Part of the problem is that the original Hebrew didn't use punctuation, so when a passage is translated, it would be very easy for the translation to convey an idea that wasn't originally intended.

To add to the problem, preachers and other religious "experts" tend to interpret scripture to the best of their understanding, so that, while we are growing up, we hear the scripture explained the same way, repeatedly. We tend to think that this explanation is correct because we've heard it so often.

But what if that interpretation is wrong? How do we know what God is really saying? This is the reason it's important to have a personal relationship with God. If God is the same, yesterday, today, and tomorrow, then everything he says must connect. He can't be a forgiving God in one part of the Bible and a harsh, demanding God in another. The truth is that he's probably somewhere in the middle.

Have you ever opened your Bible and read the scripture that your eye first falls on? Does it sometimes spark a chord in you? Or you're reading the Bible and suddenly you read a scripture that speaks to you, and you read it again? I think that these moments are God speaking to you through his word. If you ask God to explain what you're reading, thoughts will form in your mind. Sometimes the thoughts are: "This doesn't make any sense!" and sometimes the thoughts are: "This finally makes sense!"

Many people will tell you that God doesn't speak to people anymore, but I think that God has never stopped speaking to people. Some people have just stopped listening. God may not speak to me the same way that he speaks to you, but he speaks nonetheless! We may hear a song or see a sunset or overhear a conversation that resonates within us. Don't listen to people when they tell you that God only speaks in the storm or the tempest—or even in the quiet of morning. God speaks to you always—in all ways!

If you reply when he talks to you, God will have a conversation with you! You may find that God can be your very best friend—giving you the best advice you could ever get!

A Blessing for February

"May God our Father himself and our Master Jesus clear the road to you! And may the Master pour on the love so it fills your lives and splashes over on everyone around you, just as it does from us to you. May you be infused with strength and purity, filled with confidence in the presence of God our Father when our Master Jesus arrives with all his followers" (1 Thessalonians 3:11–13).

Occasionally, especially after a long, hard month, it's nice to have a special blessing. This is a great blessing to receive in February, after a long January!

Have you ever looked at the road of your life that has brought you here? Looking back, you can see where you turned left when you should have turned right. You can see the things that you thought would turn out badly, but they turned out great! You can also see where you put together all these great plans, only to have them explode in your face.

With memories of your past, it's hard to look into the future! About the time when we finally gain wisdom, we lose a lot of confidence because there have been too many unexpected turns in the road.

May the road ahead of you become clear for you to see. It's unlikely to be free of thorns and slippery rocks but, as you approach those thorny patches and those rocks that roll beneath your feet, may the hand of God lift you up so that your vision remains as clear as a glass of fresh water.

There will always be people who will say one thing even while they are doing another. People will be people, no matter what. Some people don't know any better than to lie, cheat, and steal to get what they think they want. When those people come into your life, may God's love fill you so full that you won't need their attention! When we know how much God loves us, who cares what others think? They can blow their smoke at you, but it won't matter. You are loved just as you are! May the joy of God's love overflow your life and splash on the people around you so that you live in a world of peace and beauty!

May God become so much a part of you that you have the strength to follow the path that God has set out for you! May you see his pride and his joy in you! May you move confidently into your future, knowing that God holds you in the palm of his hand and will deliver you to the destiny he has planned for you.

May blessings follow you throughout the days ahead!

There Are Preachers, and There Are Preachers

"We stand in Christ's presence when we speak; God looks us in the face. We get what we say straight from God and say it as honestly as we can" (2 Corinthians 2:17).

There are some preachers who stand behind a pulpit in a robe and proclaim God's word using mighty words and dramatic gestures. There are some preachers who stand in front of a gathering with blue jeans and tennis shoes and speak in analogies or parables.

There are preachers who work in large offices with soft carpets, beautiful artwork, and large libraries. There are preachers who work on street corners with cement floors, graffiti as their artwork, and no books in sight. Some preachers can speak for hours, and some preachers only take fifteen minutes or less.

There was a question asked some time ago about when God stopped talking to people. I happen to believe that God talks to people all the time. We sometimes don't take the time to look for him or to listen for his words.

When someone stands up in front of other people to speak what is in his mind or in his heart, I believe God enters that moment. If God has something to say to us, he looks us in the face—eye-to-eye. He speaks to our hearts, and when we try to tell someone else about what we heard – we try to tell it honestly, but sometimes our words don't convey what our hearts are telling us.

Sometimes the best sermons don't come from a person standing in front of a crowd. Sometimes the best sermons come from the silence around us. We can hear a song that we've heard for years but somehow, this time you hear it, it has a special meaning. We can hear the words this time, and they can speak to the hurting places inside us.

There can be something spiritual about the flight of the geese during fall or spring. The great migrations of birds or butterflies are amazing. No one knows why they start their journeys when they do. Sometimes young birds or butterflies will start a migration, and they haven't had any parents around to teach them where to go or when to start.

The movement of the stars and the sounds that we're able to pick up from space can speak to us. How do they know where they are going? Is there some purpose to their movements or their sounds? Planting a garden or painting a picture, singing a song, or sculpting in stone can preach sermons to our souls that the most famous preachers could never do.

Listen! Stand quietly and listen to the world around you. Can you hear the whisper of God? He's singing a love song to you!

Don't Worry, Be Happy

"As they continued down the road, they came to a stream of water. The eunuch said, 'Here's water, why can't I be baptized?' He ordered the chariot to stop. They both went down to the water, and Phillip baptized him on the spot. When they came up out of the water, the Spirit of God suddenly took Phillip off and that was the last the eunuch saw of him. But he didn't mind. He had what he'd come for and went on down the road as happy as he could be" (Acts 8:36).

This is part of a story about the disciple Phillip. The Holy Spirit told Phillip to walk over to a deserted road and, while Phillip was walking, he met up with a fellow who was trying to figure out the book of Isaiah. The Spirit told Phillip to start talking with this fellow, so they started up a conversation which led to the fellow's conversion. They happened to be passing a stream of water, and the fellow asked to be baptized.

The water didn't have any special prayers said over it; it was good water, direct from God. It didn't matter who the fellow was, except that he'd asked to be baptized. When they came up out of the stream, Phillip disappeared, but the fellow wasn't too worried over this experience. It seems that he was content with what he had and went merrily on his way.

In 2007, there was a song sung by Bobby McFerrin called "Don't Worry, Be Happy!" It was quite a hit song, and a lot of people quoted the title, smiling as they did so.

There are a lot of sober-minded people who feel that they need to worry over everything, and possibly they should. They are the people who have portfolios and plan meals for the month. They have coordinated outfits and make sure that they attend all the right functions, shaking all the right hands. These are important things to do and to have, and I don't want to diminish them.

I do, however, want to suggest that there is also a need for people who don't have portfolios and who don't plan their meals. We need people who dress adventurously and don't attend any functions at all. We need people who don't care who you are when they shake your hand. We need people who are happy to get what they came for and to move on down the road.

There is something about a beautifully appointed church with candles lit, sunlight streaming through the stained-glass windows, and the organ playing. It can feed our souls to see people filling the pews and worshipping God. The beauty of the surroundings enhances the experience—it doesn't create the experience.

There is something about a spot in nature, with nobody around—just you and God. There may be trees, mountains, oceans, or even an open plain. There may be animals or a gentle breeze. There may be a storm on the way with the wind blowing the minor frets from your mind. The beauty of the surroundings enhances the experience—it doesn't create the experience.

Know that however you worship God, the important thing is God—not where you worship!

How Do We Know What We Believe?

"Dear Friend, when you extend hospitality to Christian brothers and sisters, even when they are strangers, you make the faith visible" (3 John 5).

According to *The American Heritage Dictionary of the English Language* (published by American Heritage Publishing Co. and Houghton Mifflin Company, with a copyright date of 1969), a single word threads itself through all the definitions of "faith"—belief. If we have faith in the edibility of Mom's apple pie, then we believe that it will always be good to eat. In reality, Mom's pies aren't always the same—some days they are better than others—but to us, her pies will always be the best. If we have faith in the veracity of a particular person, we will believe that person is telling us the truth—as he knows it in that moment.

If we want to know where our faith lies, a good indicator is in looking at our beliefs. I have found that, to discover what we truly believe, we need to look at our actions.

For example, I have always believed that I was a patient person—until I found myself trying to make a deposit in an ATM machine. It asked me to confirm my deposit information, and by the time I had pushed the "confirm" button ten times, I discovered that I didn't have as much patience as I had thought. People in the line next to me were looking at me askance and moving quietly away from me.

We all know people who smile broadly at those around them, they shake hands when they see you, and ask about your family—presenting themselves as friendly people that we should feel comfortable with.

Oftentimes, those who proclaim their goodness the loudest will have large crowds around them, but their actions will not always confirm their proclamations. They can (and will) be consistently rude to others, overlooking people in their rush to be "the best with the most."

On the other hand, we all know people who don't make much fuss. They stand quietly in the background watching others. If they see a child about to be knocked out of the way by the rush of crowds, they calmly take the child's hand and remove themselves to safety. If they see someone nearby who is alone, they strike up a conversation, creating a connection.

If you want to see what a person truly believes, watch how they behave. Do they help the elderly find comfortable seating? Do they hold doors open for others or help carry their burdens? How do they behave around children?

For that matter, do you ever look at your own behaviors? Socrates is supposed to have said, "The unexamined life is not worth living." Occasionally, it's a good idea to look back at your life—how you reacted in different situations. Were you brave enough to stand up for someone being persecuted? Did you watch while someone behaved badly toward another? We profess our faith with every action taken. You may want to look back to see what you believed and how you have evolved. You might be pleasantly surprised!

Bragging Rights

"If I have to 'brag' about myself, I'll brag about the humiliations that make me like Jesus. The eternal and blessed God and Father of our Master Jesus knows I'm not lying" (2 Corinthians 11:30–31).

Some people will take credit for everything that works. According to them, they hung the sun in the sky and tilted the world to create the seasons. They order the affairs of men so that good stuff will be the result. Their eloquence stops wars and rules the country. These are the people that bring out the worst in me. I want to punch them in the nose, but even that reaction doesn't bother them. To them, it confirms their opinion of my intelligence level. There isn't much to be done with them. The world will have to whack them upside the head a few times before they understand.

Some people have done one thing in their lives, but that one thing was spectacular. These are the people for whom plaques are added to buildings or signs are placed outside of towns to notify the visitors that someone did something special there. Someone won the world's trapshooting trophy or someone else developed a vaccine for polio. These are great things, and they add to the world, but the world is more than trapshooting or developing one cure for one disease. The thing about most of these people is that they are usually very humble. They tend to put their trophies or certificates in a drawer or on their walls, but you don't hear about these triumphs ten times a day. These people can be a joy to be around because they are interested in a lot of things—not just sports or chemistry.

I read somewhere that most geniuses enjoy good health and have a lot of friends. They tend to be well rounded so that they can talk with almost anybody on almost any topic. They are interested in a lot of things, and they know how to listen.

There is a saying, "People don't care how much you know until they know how much you care." People have a great need to be seen and heard. They need to have confirmation that they have value. Those braggarts who claim to have done everything have an overwhelming need to receive value from other people. How sad that would be, to be so undervalued by yourself that you must tell everyone of your great deeds—continuously!

If you want to change the world—or even if you just want to survive the day—one way to do so is to connect with other people. Instead of offering solutions for everyone else's problems, try talking about something that bothers you, whether it's a messy house, screaming kids, or even whether to wear a mask in public. There will be someone who joins with you in your concerns, and the next thing you know, your heart won't be so heavy. You may even find a cure for the problems of the world! Now that would be something to brag about!

The Building vs. the Builder

"A builder is more valuable than a building any day. Every house has a builder but the Builder behind them all is God" (Hebrews 3:3b–4).

The idea is that animate beings have more value than inanimate objects. I don't think that anyone would argue with this. People would certainly have more value than a can of olives or a box of facial tissues (although, when I have a runny nose, boxes of tissues are important). But we sometimes have close attachments to specific inanimate objects. Maybe it has to do with the associations we make with inanimate objects. Macaroni and cheese is an especially important comfort food for me, but it doesn't taste quite right unless I have a can of peaches to go with it. And what is a hamburger without the accompanying fries?

OK, so maybe food as an inanimate object isn't a good example. Many of us have strong ties to our food. Many of us have strong ties to our first vehicle. Do you remember the house you grew up in or the first piece of furniture you bought?

I think that inanimate objects have great value depending on the memories we associate with them; but when we die and no longer have those associations, the objects lose their value. Unfortunately, it seems that animate beings (pets, house plants, … people) can sometimes do the same thing. People who once had a great impact on our lives, when we move away and no longer see them every day, can become buried in our memories. Only when we go through a box of pictures, and we see them smiling out of a photograph do we remember the joy we had with them, and we wonder where they are now.

The builder of a house determines where the rooms are in that house—where the kitchen will be or the bathroom. How many bedrooms or closets? Will there be a separate dining room or perhaps a family room?

If you consider yourself your own house, how will you build it? How will you care for it? Will it have value for you? Will the kitchen of your mind send out good food that nourishes you, or will it only focus on the cookies and cakes that taste good for the moment but never satisfy? Will the family room of your heart be large enough to hold a lot of people or will there only be room enough for one or two people?

It's an interesting concept, isn't it? The idea of building yourself as your own house. It might not hurt to bring in an expert builder. You couldn't ask for a better expert than God. Just saying.

What Else Do We Need?

"Our God gives you everything you need, makes you everything you're to be" (2 Thessalonians 1:2).

One of the problems that I have in praying to be healed is that God has such an odd sense of humor that, while I know I'll be healed, I'm not too sure exactly what will be healed or what I'll have to go through to be healed.

I remember that for a while, I was praying for mighty blessings. I got a lot of blessings, but they were intangible blessings, like good cheer, good friends I could turn to in times of trouble, family who would come to my aid when I was getting ready to move back home, a roof over my head, clothes on my back, and food in my belly. I gained a better grasp of innovation and creativity but not a lot of money. God answered my prayer in spades, but I would just as soon have gotten the cash.

Praying to be healed is a lot like praying for blessings. I have prayed to be healed when I came down with cataracts, and I was healed—of a feeling of urgency to go places. I think I'm being healed of impatience, but the jury is still out on that.

I do believe God gives us everything we need, but that doesn't always match up with what we think we need. I heard someone talking about how, if you ask specifically for certain things like money or healing of your broken foot, God will provide it, but you must be specific, and you must have enough faith. But Luke 17:6 tells us that we just need faith the size of a mustard seed. The problem I have with this is that it doesn't always work the way you think it will. I've prayed for enough money to cover my expenses only to receive the answer, "Don't live so high on the hog!"

I believe that God provides for his children in many amazing ways. I also believe that if we'll let him, he'll polish us up until we shine. The thing that I tend to forget is that the sandpaper or metal files used to start the polishing process are all rough. We can get really scraped up at the start but, if we hang in there, the final polishing cloths are soft and fine.

I believe that faith is in the choices we make. I knew a fellow in college who was a summer lifeguard. He told me once that sometimes, when rescuing someone who's drowning, the person being saved will start to panic and will strike out at the person trying to save them. It's easier to rescue an unconscious person because you can move them around so that they are more aerodynamic and can move through the water more easily.

That's like my faith walk. When I focus on the problems in front of me, I struggle to help God with lots of great suggestions. When I leave it all to God, the problems will be solved in wonderful ways.

May you have a blessed Advent season!

What Do We Do with This?

"Herod, when he realized that the scholars had tricked him, flew into a rage. He commanded the murder of every little boy two years old and under who lived in Bethlehem and its surrounding hills" (Matthew 2:16).

The birth of Christ is filled with difficulties starting before he's born. Mary must agree to have God's son, Joseph must decide whether to marry Mary, and the newly married couple must travel a long way because someone in politics decided to find out who was living in their district (and who could pay more taxes)!

We have a *very* pregnant Mary and Joseph, traveling on a donkey (probably a used donkey with faulty suspension) to Bethlehem and finding that all the motels are full (and the hotels and the bed-and-breakfasts). They find a place in a stable with lots of animals, and this is where Jesus is born.

The shepherds come for a visit, and the wise men come bringing the first Christmas presents. The story should end well with a tender lullaby playing in the background while the camera closes in on a beautiful baby boy.

But that isn't the end of the story about the birth of Jesus. After the visit of the wise men, Matthew adds this strange little postscript. Why did he have to include the tragedy of these little ones who died just because Jesus was born?

I think that one of the hardest things to bear would be the death of a child, particularly the death of your own child. How can we find a reason for this? What kind of God would allow a child to be born with any kind of difficulties, much less allow a child to die?

I have no answers, but I do know that tragedy is a part of life. No one gets through life without experiencing at least one tragic moment. I also know that when horror strikes, and we are swept off our feet, we need to talk about it. Not to just anyone, but to someone who loves us and cares about us. We need to be able to pound our fists into the ground and to cry out to the heavens. If we don't share the experience with someone, we are diminishing the person we lost.

I believe that God cares for all his creation from the ground on which we walk to the stars that inhabit the skies. I believe that God loves each of us with a love that is unfathomable. I believe that God knows everything that's happening in the universe, and I believe that he sees our sorrow and he grieves with us. I believe that he sees our joys and rejoices with us. I don't know if God causes all things to happen or if he allows it, but I believe that he is with us in everything we're going through. If you need a listening ear, you couldn't ask for a better one than his.

Who's Your Best Friend?

"Seek good and not evil—and live! You talk about God-of-the-Angel-Armies being your best friend. Well, LIVE like it, and maybe it will happen" (Amos 5:14).

What makes a best friend? My best friend is one who's stuck with me for a long time. When I moved away, she called and wrote me letters to keep me updated on what was going on. When I moved back, we went out to celebrate.

She doesn't know all the same people I know, although she knows a lot of them. We don't always agree on everything. We argue over stuff. I like cartoons, and she likes reality shows. She's an elegant lady, and I'm usually dressed in men's jeans, oversized socks, and tennis shoes, with a man's T-shirt. She likes to tell me that I'm not a man, and I need to wear women's clothing. Occasionally, I'll put on a girls' shirt just for her.

When good things happened, like when I got a job or met a great fellow, I could call her, and she'd be as excited as I was. When my folks died, she was one of the first people I called, and she sat by me—not speaking, just joining in my sorrow. When people treat me unfairly, she's in my corner—always on my side (even as we argue over what I'm going to wear when I kick them in the shins). She shares her family with me and makes sure that I'm not alone on holidays. She remembers my birthday.

Our best friends are those who give of themselves. Whether or not they give expensive gifts is immaterial. They give their time, their attention, their presence.

One of the things I like most about this growing trend toward minimalism is that we're discovering that joy and happiness don't come from things. We can't buy true friendship. We invest time and care in our friends. We pay attention to them. We hurt when they hurt, and we celebrate with them. We think of them and, while we may not always remember their birthday, we remember the month they were born in. We know that they like sweet stories and soft fabrics.

Our best friend ever was born a long time ago. He wasn't on this earth very long, and yet his life extends from the beginning to the end. He rules over the universe and yet he knows you. He sees you in the morning when you first wake up. With your hair standing on end and drool coming from your mouth, while you struggle to open your eyes, he looks at you and says, "I love you." When darkness comes into your life, he'll enfold you in his love and walk with you through it. He will never leave you alone for richer or for poorer, in sickness and in health, and death cannot part you!

Wishing you a warm, wonderful Christmas, however you may be spending it!

I've Got This

"On the Big Day, I'll look after everyone who lives in Jerusalem so that the lowliest, weakest person will be as glorious as David and the family of David itself will be godlike, like the Angel of God leading the people" (Zechariah 12:8).

There will come a day, says Zechariah, when all the countries surrounding Israel will turn against the Israelites, and Israel will come under attack. God, however, says not to worry—he has it covered.

The question that begs to be asked, however, is have there been many times when Israel wasn't under attack? It seems like God's people have been under attack ever since God chose them. When Abraham first came to Canaan, he was beset by people already living there. A couple of times he had to pretend that his wife was his sister so that the head of the country wouldn't kill Abraham to get Sarah.

Then there was Isaac, Abraham's son, who had the same problem. Jacob's own brother tried to do him in, and Jacob had to run away to his uncle's house. God's chosen people have been under attack in one way or another since the very beginning, and yet, have you noticed that they are still here?

It turns out, in 2017, it was calculated that 22.4 percent of the Nobel Prizes were won by Jews even though they make up less than .2 percent of the world's population. It seems that someone is indeed watching over the house of Abraham. In 2019, over 65 percent of the Nobel Prizes were won by Christians and, in 2010, Christians accounted for about 31.6 percent of the world's population.

The Good News is that, because of Jesus, we are adopted into Abraham's family and covered by all the promises God made to Israel, but we don't have to make the living sacrifices! The sacrifices were to cover our sins so that the people of God could come into his presence. God sent a pattern for living that would mark his people as holy, but no one could maintain that pattern on their own. That's why so many sacrifices were required.

Jesus became the sacrifice for us. When Jesus came to earth and became human, he was able to meet all the requirements for holiness. Believing in him, we are putting on his holiness so that we can come before God, the Father.

That doesn't mean that we'll come out without some bumps and bruises (and sometimes we'll come out with some major trauma—just ask the Jews) but it does mean that, in the end, God has us covered. This doesn't mean that we are perfect. It means that Jesus loved us so much that he was willing to take on our sins so that we could have access to the God of the universe. And that makes Jesus the best Christmas present ever!

Here's wishing you a happy new year. May it be filled with hope, joy, and peace—and not too many bumps and bruises!

We're Fine, but I Can't Say the Same about the Ship

"From now on, things are looking up! I can assure you that there'll not be a single drowning among us, although I can't say as much for the ship—the ship itself is doomed" (Acts 27:22).

(Author's note: This was written in early January 2021, not long after the January 6 raid on Congress. Americans had been dealing with the confusion of the pandemic reports and the reports of violence throughout the country. Those reports were conflicting also. Some indicated that the people who died were ordinary people trying to live their lives in peace while some reports indicated that those who died were not the upstanding citizens they were made out to be. There was a lot of anger and confusion in our society and some talk about what would happen to the country in which we live.)

After Paul was seized in the temple in Jerusalem and taken to the Roman authorities, he was sent to Rome for a hearing before Caesar. Sailing west from Jerusalem, they stopped at different places on the way, and at one point they encountered a storm that blew them off course.

Paul gathers everyone on the ship and tells them that, if they stayed together, they would all be safe. This scripture is part of his speech to those people. The ship was able to get close to land before it started to break apart. Those who could swim jumped overboard, and those who couldn't swim found planks they could hang on to. Everyone made it to land, but the ship broke apart on the reefs off the coast.

It's strange, when I think about it, that we put so much faith in things. We like to travel so we buy cars to take us places in comfort. We like to sleep so we buy sleeping surfaces that will provide the type of sleep we're looking for—whether it is a cot in a tent, pillow-top mattresses, sofas, or recliners. Most of the stuff we buy is to provide us with a good experience of some kind.

It isn't just tangible things we look for. The people we marry are chosen because we think that they'll help us build the families we want. We choose jobs that will provide security, status, adventure, safety, whatever.

When we choose a car or a job or a life partner, and the result isn't as good as we expected, it's scary. It hits us in our concept of ourselves. We think we are good judges of what we're looking for and, when our choice doesn't live up to our expectations, it throws doubt on our judgment.

Between the pandemic, the politics, the race riots, and the general violence that is going on in our country, it's scary to think that the ship of our government may develop deep cracks and the water may flood parts of it. The riot in our nation's capital was shocking to hear about and to watch. We are not the kind of people who would storm the buildings in which our government does its business. While we have had warriors who have become instrumental in our government, we don't think of our country's leaders as being warriors.

In the final analysis, however, our country was founded by warriors. We fought oceans, harsh weather, diseases, and ourselves to become who we are. Somehow, no matter what happens to the ship we're in, Americans will survive all the "slings and arrows of outrageous fortune" and come out safely on the other side. I believe that's called faith!

Take Heart

"In this godless world you will continue to experience difficulties. But take heart! I've conquered the world" (John 16:33).

(Author's note: This was written in February 2021. There were fewer deaths due to COVID-19 but there were deaths due to violence in our communities. To make matters worse, our climate was changing so that the forecasts that we were used to were being replaced by extreme temperatures. We were being faced by the fragility of life in ways that we couldn't ignore. We were each, in our own way, looking for some stability and some hope for the future.)

This scripture is from the passage during the Last Supper when Jesus talks honestly with his disciples about what is to come. These are the men who have stood with Jesus through thick and thin. They were there when Jesus was run out of synagogues and when he was treated like a king. These are Jesus's friends of the heart.

When I was a little girl, my folks would leave for a weekend about once or twice a year, going to conventions in Wichita or Kansas City and they would always get a babysitter to come and stay with my brother and me. Before the folks headed out on their trip, there would be long discussions on what needed to happen when, and how this or that situation could best be handled. We all heaved a great sigh of relief when Mom and Dad finally closed the car doors and headed down the driveway.

This is, in a way, what Jesus was doing. He was going to be gone for an extended time, and he wanted to prepare his brothers-of-the-heart for what lay ahead of them. There would be great joy, great heartache, and great difficulties, but through it all, Jesus would be there with them just as he is here with us now.

This has been such a difficult eleven months. It seemed like everything was changing daily for a while last year. Between the pandemic and the politics and the violence, we all seemed to curl in on ourselves. It's starting to get a little better, or maybe we're just getting tired of living with the sense of panic that flourished there for a while. Businesses are finding ways to accommodate the customers who are afraid to go through their doors as well as those who refuse to wear masks. We are slowly starting to find ways to reconnect with family and friends.

And now, it seems that the weather wants to get into the act. We're encouraged to limit our contact with other people who may have the coronavirus, but now we don't want to leave our houses because the temperatures are below 0° F. If we don't die of the COVID, we'll freeze to death by the side of the road.

Jesus knew what he was saying when he warned the disciples over two thousand years ago that there would be difficulties in this world. In fact, that is a rather good understatement. People have been having difficulties with life ever since we left the Garden of Eden.

Jesus also knew what he was saying when he told us to take heart—to not become discouraged. In one of the first "spoiler alerts," Jesus gave away the end of the story when he told us that he had overcome the world. If we can keep putting one foot in front of the other, through Jesus Christ, we win in the end!

A Holy Terror

"God will be seen as truly terrible—a Holy Terror. All earth-made gods will shrivel up and blow away, and everyone, wherever they are, far or near, will fall to the ground and worship him" (Zephaniah 2:11).

Zephaniah talks about how God's children need to get back with him because there's going to come a time when God decides to clean house and then, Katie-bar-the-door because God will get down to business! I'm finding, however, that this scripture brings a kind of comfort for today.

We have all known those people who deliberately cause dissension! There is no way to pretty them up! They are rude, crude, and all-around disgusting. They think they own the very sidewalks they walk on and stride down the middle—probably on their cell phones, making important deals. They never listen to what you say, and when they finally acknowledge your presence, they dismiss you with a sneer. They foreclose on widows and orphans and celebrate with their friends afterward. They raise puppies and chickens to train them to fight, and they probably run off to Africa to kill baby elephants.

These are the people who make me so mad! I want to smash their faces in or break their kneecaps or destroy their lives. My problem is that, usually, when I try to pay them back for the rotten things they do—it all comes back on me. I try to tell others about the rotten things these people have done, and I come out looking like a gossipmonger out to destroy an innocent person's reputation!

At these times, this scripture comes to my mind. I can close my eyes and see God standing in front of me facing these rotten people who are up to no good. His eyes flash fire, and half of them fall to the ground in flames, writhing in pain. He opens his mouth, and the other half clamp their hands to their ears because their brains are overloading with horror.

I can sit back down again because, once I've given these rotten people to God, I can let them go and know that they will be paid for their actions in ways beyond my imagining. God can individualize each punishment for these people to reach maximum destruction, and he can lengthen their lives so that they live in misery for a long time.

I don't think of myself as particularly violent, but some people can bring out the creativity in me! It's better for me to leave it all to God! He's so subtle about some things. Sometimes the punishment is a long marriage to a miserable partner or a shipwreck at sea where the rotten person is confined to a tropical island with no electricity and no cell phone! Maybe God will give me a glimpse of their suffering, and I can rejoice and thank him quietly.

God is the best secret weapon ever!

Who's in Charge, Anyway?

"The God who made the world and everything in it, this Master of sky and land doesn't live in custom-made shrines or need the human race to run errands for him, as if he couldn't take care of himself. He makes the creatures; the creatures don't make him" (Acts 17:24–25).

Some time ago, I heard a comment about God that really stopped me cold. It takes a lot to silence me, but this comment did the trick. This lady was talking about church and how we need to be careful to protect the presence of God. I think she was talking about respecting God and how we need to treat him with reverential awe, and she had a point. My problem is that I sometimes hear—far off in the distance, like an overheard conversation—how we need to be careful around God. The implication is that God can't handle reality.

I believe that God made us to begin with—not just the prototype but each of us individually. When you're making anything, usually you start with the insides first. If you're building a house, you start planning with the rooms you need and where they should be located. If you're making a bed, you start with the sheets—not the covers. God knows what is inside each of us—the secret places of our hearts and minds. He knows what motivates us and how we "tick."

I'm not sure which public relations firm first presented the idea that God is so delicate and fragile that he can't handle the daily lives that we lead, but it should win an award for most people influenced by an idea. Heaven forbid that God should hear how we cut in front of a little old lady at the store because we didn't have time to wait on her. We want to make sure that everyone hears how we tithe every week to our church, but we don't want anyone (especially God) to hear how we're padding our expense accounts.

If we believe that God lives within our hearts, shouldn't we expect him to hear about what we're doing—even in the quiet places of our minds? God tells us to bring everything to him and to "lean not unto our own understanding" but to expect him to take care of us. Jesus told us that if God can clothe the lilies in beautiful outfits and if he can take care of the birds in the air, why wouldn't he do the same with us.

While there are some parents who don't pay any attention to their kids, God is not one of those parents. He is actively involved in our lives, whether we want him to be or not. We are not the parent trying to raise God to be a responsible adult. God is the Master of the universe, trying to raise us up to be loving children of his.

What Did You Say?

"Words are powerful; take them seriously" (Matthew 12:37).

Have you ever said something that you thought was clever and had people look at you like you had just taken your clothes off in public? With my shiny new diploma in hand, I went for my first interview as a teacher. In touring the school, I mentioned that I thought it was "really cool"—meaning "I liked it." The principal who was interviewing me said that he was sorry, they had just turned the air conditioning on and perhaps the temperature was a bit low. I then had to explain what I had meant, and the whole thing became awkward. I was not surprised when I didn't get the job.

One of the difficult things about any language—including English—is that words often have multiple meanings. Some of those meanings are diametrically opposed to each other. I can be "behind" you all the way (meaning that I agree with you and will stand with you in a fight). I can be "behind" you, watching every move (meaning that I don't trust you and will be checking to see what you do). I can be "behind" in my deadlines (meaning that I'm running late and not following my schedule). That doesn't even consider the words we say when we're teasing or being sarcastic.

The story is told about a lady who texted her son to let him know that an uncle had died. She ended the text with "lol." The son called her and asked why she was laughing because this uncle had died. She didn't understand his question. She wasn't laughing; she was signing off the way she signed off on her letters, "lots of love." She was just saving space in her text.

I was talking with my brother and his wife after Dad passed away. We were talking about some things that had stories around them, like an old, silver-plated vase that Dad had resilvered. I hadn't seen it in the house, and I had asked them if they had it, which they did. A comment was made to the effect that because it had been resilvered, it had no value. I replied that all things have value; after which there was an odd silence that I didn't understand until much later when I realized that they were talking about monetary value, and I was talking about sentimental value. Sometimes those misunderstandings can create deep wounds that take years to heal.

Misunderstandings over the words we use can occur over anything from unimportant to crucial conversations. In this passage from Matthew, Jesus is saying that our words come from our hearts and can reveal our true thoughts. The sad thing is that sometimes God is the only one who can interpret our words correctly. We listen to what is being said, but what we hear is filtered through our experiences. Unless we really know the person speaking, we may not understand what is being said.

In Closing

After God created people with a free will, he called his Breath and his Word to him. Getting everyone a cup of coffee, God joined them at the kitchen table. His concern was that people would become fascinated by all the shiny objects to be found in the world. If they became more interested in chasing after these than in fixing their eyes on him, they might get lost. God was worried that they might not be able to find their way back to him.

Breath and Word looked at each other for a moment and then God's Word spoke up. Taking a deep breath, he offered to provide an Easter to guide God's children back home, but he would like to have a Christmas first so that they could get to know him personally.

God smiled and thanked him.

And so the Word became flesh and dwelt among men. We know him as Jesus.

Printed in the United States
by Baker & Taylor Publisher Services